WHY BUBBLES ARE GREAT

FOR THE ECONOMY

DANIEL GROSS

 Collins

An Imprint of HarperCollinsPublishers

FIRST EDITION

Designed by Jaime Putorti

Library of Congress Cataloging-in-Publication Data
Gross, Daniel
  Pop! : why bubbles are great for the economy / Daniel Gross. — 1st ed.
    p.   cm.
  Includes bibliographical references.
  ISBN: 978-0-06-115154-5
  ISBN-10: 0-06-115154-8
    1. Investments.   2. Stocks.   3. Bull markets.   4. Bear markets.
  5. Speculation.   6. Business cycles.   I. Title.

HG4521.G743 2007
332.6—dc22   2007060506

07 08 09 10 11 DIX/RRD 10 9 8 7 6 5 4 3 2 1

To Aliza and Ethan

CONTENTS

BUBBLES "R" US

Oops! . . . I did it again.

—BRITNEY SPEARS, MAY 2000

On October 9, 2006, with the Dow hovering near a record 12,000, the markets got a jolt. Google, the eight-year-old money machine, announced it would buy YouTube, the eighteen-month-old Web video-sharing phenomenon, for $1.65 billion in stock.

Uh-oh. Stocks at multiyear highs. A young tech company using its high-flying stock to snarf up, at a seemingly outrageous valuation, a company with little revenues but gazillions of eyeballs. (YouTube held its financials closely but loudly trumpeted the 100 million videos viewed daily at the site.) The positive reaction in the stock market. (Google's stock rose 8.5 points on the news, creating enough new value to make the transaction essentially free.) The rumors and gossip surrounding the acquisition target's also-ran peers, like Facebook. "It sounds like a tale from the late 1990's dot-com bubble," wrote astute deal observer Andrew Ross Sorkin in the *New York Times*. Less astute deal observer Matt Lauer seconded the notion, opening the October 11 *Today* show with this irresistible teaser: "Bubblicious. Could Google's billion-dollar purchase of YouTube signal another dot-com boom?"

Bollocks.

Despite the media's rush to portray the deal as a return to the glory days of 1999, before Lauer's hairline and

CNBC's ratings had receded so dramatically, the Google-YouTube tie-up emphatically did not herald a return of the dot-com bubble. Rather, it was a logical and historically resonant *result* of the 1990s bubble. Google, the dork-powered cream of the Web 2.0 crop, was founded in 1998, gained critical mass amid the postbust tristesse, went public in August 2004, and instantly took flight. Superior search algorithms account for Google's astonishing performance and profitability. The stock market valued Google that day at about $128 billion—more than it did most components of the Dow Jones Industrial Average. And while the company used about 2 percent of its high-flying stock as currency, Google could have simply written a check. It had about $9.8 billion in cash and marketable securities on its balance sheet.

But all that code would have been worthless if not for the excess human and technological capacity surrounding the Internet that was created in the 1990s. Google prospered by hiring engineers and computer scientists, many of whom had been made redundant after the bust; by lashing together hundreds of thousands of cheap servers; by tapping into an installed base of 172 million U.S. Web surfers, many whom enjoyed zippy broadband connections; by selling ads to hundreds of thousands of online advertisers desperate for leads, links, and clicks; and by placing ads on blogs and social networking sites.

YouTube, which went from zero to 100 million videos

per day in the time it takes an infant to learn to walk, was likewise built on infrastructure laid down in the 1990s. Without near-universal broadband (ever try streaming a video over a 56K dial-up modem?) and the spread of what *Forbes* publisher Rich Karlgaard calls the continuing "cheap revolution" in technology, teens would not be able to make videos on their PCs and digital cameras, upload them to the Net quickly, and post links on their MySpace pages. There's much more to the Web 2.0 phenomenon than Google and YouTube: the virtual universe Second Life; Wi-Fi networks; the burgeoning blogging industry; iTunes; the $211.4 billion e-commerce juggernaut, growing at 20 percent per year; and the $16 billion online advertising industry. Next, add the macroeconomic numbers that are more difficult to crunch. How much cash do corporations save each year due to falling data transmission and storage costs? What's the value of the time saved—and hence money earned— from instant messaging, file sharing, BlackBerrys, the online phone service Skype, ordering groceries online through Peapod, using Google to conduct research, and outsourcing insurance claims processing to Bangalore? In the years since the bubble burst in 2000, the way Americans work and communicate has changed dramatically, in large part because the technological infrastructure laid down in the 1990s has been put to such remarkable use.

The cycle seen in fiber optics and dot-coms in the 1990s and the early part of this decade—a burst of frantic building and excess capacity, outlandish hype, and cutthroat price competition, bankruptcy and consolidation, self-pity and finger-pointing, short-term losses for many and long-term gains for everybody—is nothing new. Similar manias and bubbles surrounded other promising economic and technological developments: the telegraph in the 1840s and 1850s, the railroads in the 1880s and 1890s, stocks and credit in the 1920s. These bubbles, and their contribution to America's remarkable record of economic growth and innovation, are the subject of this book.

•

What's an investment bubble? There's no satisfying textbook definition. But it goes something like this. In every generation, people arise to proclaim that a new technology or a new set of economic assumptions and financial tools promise untold riches. The new, new thing will both alter history and free us from its musty grasp. As a result, the old rules simply no longer apply. Promoters concoct pro forma numbers that extrapolate impressive short-term trends indefinitely into the future. Evangelists and proselytizers urge people to abandon reason and steady habits, and browbeat those who steadfastly stick to their sense of rationality. As telecom promoter George Gilder put it in a December 31, 1999, premillennial op-ed in the *Wall Street Journal*, "The investor who never acts until the financials affirms his choice is doomed to mediocrity by trust in spurious rationality." Yes, there are always some fuddy-duddy doubters. In 1995, surveying an unfolding investment craze in a new technology, one pessimist wrote: "A few will pay off, but when the frenzy is behind us, we will look back incredulously at the wreckage of failed venture and wonder, 'Who funded those companies? What was going on in their minds?' " But, hey, what does Microsoft founder Bill Gates know about new technologies that George Gilder doesn't?

As the bubble takes shape, a chorus of pundits, shills, and true believers concoct eminently solid reasons why this time is different. The authors of the 1999 howler *Dow 36,000*, James Glassman and Kevin Hassett, and Irving Fisher, the Yale economist who in 1929 proclaimed that "stock prices have reached what looks like a permanently high plateau," genuinely believed that the nation stood on the verge of a new era. So did Henry O'Reilly, whose enthusiasm for the telegraph was so great that he rounded up capital and strung up wires throughout Pennsylvania and Ohio in the 1840s, heedless of the utter lack of demand for the service. And so did David Lereah, chief economist of the National Association of Realtors, who in February 2005 published a book bearing the top-calling title *Are You Missing the Real Estate Boom? The Boom Will Not Bust and Why Property Values Will Continue to Climb Through the End of the Decade—and How to Profit from Them*. Naturally, housing prices peaked in a matter of months.

As the bubble takes flight, the sector swells to an outsize part of the economy and pushes up demand for the commodities and services it consumes. Now the phenomenon crosses over into the larger consciousness, even if only a small portion of Americans are financially caught up in it. "The striking thing about the stock market speculation of 1929 was not the massiveness of the participation," wrote John Kenneth Galbraith. "Rather it was the way it became central to the culture." I still remember, with astonishing vividness, the guys behind the counter at my rotisserie chicken place in New York watching CNBC in 1998 and holding forth about the utility of options. Meanwhile, crooks, charlatans, frauds, and mountebanks are elevated into visionaries. In his 2000 book, *Telecosm*, George Gilder predicted that Bernie Ebbers's MCI WorldCom "stands ready to release many more trillions of dollars in wealth in Internet commerce and communications and threaten monopolies around the globe. He is a hero of the dimensions of Rockefeller and Milken." (That wasn't the dumbest projection in Gilder's book. This was: "Profits will migrate toward newspapers and magazines.")

The bubble fully aloft, investors and managers are seized by pervasive me-tooism, a conviction that the fourth, fifth, and sixth movers will enjoy first-mover advantage. Every khaki-clad MBA in the dot-com era had a business plan in his pocket, arguing that if he could take just 5 percent of whatever space he happened to be in, he'd be golden. Unfortunately, fifty other khaki-clad MBAs had the exact same idea. In the United States, a good business gets funded—and then funded again and again—especially when a sector is hot. At the end of 2006, there were sixty-three ethanol refineries with a combined annual capacity of 5.4 billion gallons under construction; during 2006, total production capacity was 5.3 billion gallons. The same mentality led railroad promoters to build multiple trunk lines traversing the continent to connect business centers. Railway mileage in the United States nearly doubled between 1880 and 1890; by 1893, one-quarter of the U.S. rail system was in bankruptcy.

Meanwhile, an important parallel process takes place. During bubbles, a great deal of money and energy is spent building up the *mental infrastructure* surrounding a new technology—convincing people to invest, to use new media, to make Internet phone calls, to reserve hotel rooms by telegraph, to send grain by rail instead of by canal barge, to buy stocks and investment trusts instead of leaving cash under the mattress. Part of the madness—and brilliance—of the 1990s was the eagerness of so many companies to run businesses at negative margins in order to attract users. Kozmo.com, a New York–based courier service, would deliver a Snickers bar to your desk. Amazon.com had a business model predicated on losing money, the more the better! The competition created by excess capacity—too many e-retailers, too many fiber-optic providers, too many railroads, too many telegraphs, too many condos competing for too few customers—inevitably leads to vicious price competition that is a positive good for consumers.

Next comes the end stage. As business plans start to go sour, managers panic. They slash prices feverishly, cook the books, or just plain lie. Joseph Schumpeter, the economist who promulgated the notion of creative destruction, compared the upper strata of an entrepreneurial economy to a hotel, always full but with guests always checking in and checking out. When bubbles start to deflate, the guests at the Schumpeter Hyatt pick one another's pockets, clobber one another senseless, and then leave without paying the bill.

Finally, when economic reality catches up to dreams and hype, the bubble bursts. Pop! It's the airship *Hindenburg* at Lakehurst, New Jersey, in May 1937, a massive explosion followed by bankruptcies, declining asset values, red-faced brokers, and promotional books piling up on the remainder tables. Oh, the portfolios! Like the solid citizens of River City in *The Music Man*, hardworking and utterly gullible, we were all too eager to look beyond the obvious scam and see the potential for a tremendous wind orchestra. In the nonfiction version, however, Dr. Harold Hill doesn't stay to marry the librarian. He leaves town, gold coins spilling out of his pockets as he hops the train. As fiber-optic behemoth Global Crossing went bust in 2002, founder and CEO Gary Winnick, who sold tons of stock at the top, was puttering around his obscene $94 million residence in Bel Air. And we think: how could we be so stupid, so thick? How could we imagine that Pets.com, sending fifty-pound bags of Kibbles 'n Bits through the mail, was a viable business model? How could we join Condo Flip and use credit cards to put down payments on unbuilt Miami condos?

A period of ritualized mourning and self-flagellation worthy of the Shiite Ashura follows. Ironically, a chronically underpaid lot—journalists—finally prosper as book-length jeremiads are commissioned. And so we have a rich history of bubble literature, morality tales that highlight greed, naïveté, the tendency toward madness and criminality. "The public mind was in a state of unwholesome fermentation . . . The hope of boundless wealth for the morrow made them heedless and extravagant for today," Charles Mackay wrote of the eighteenth-century South Sea Bubble in his 1841 volume, *Memoirs of Extraordinary Popular Delusions*. John Kenneth Galbraith, in his enduring classic *The Great Crash, 1929*, described "the mass escape into make-believe, so much a part of the true speculative orgy." Roger Lowenstein's best-selling 2004 postmortem, *Origins of the Crash: The Great Bubble and Its Undoing*, flays fin de siècle America for "a mass refusal to acknowledge reason—even a mass *indifference* to reason."

It's hard not to read these books without feeling a sense of self-loathing, shame, and embarrassment, and to leave the library with a firm lesson in hand. Excessively speculative investments in fixed assets are bad—bad for investors, bad for employees of the bubble companies, and bad for the economy.

Of course they're right. But what if they're only half right? While the literature on bubbles and their piercing is deep and rich, the literature on the positive aspects of bubbles is slim. And yet. One can't help but think that the sackcloth-and-ashes approach misses part of the story. The pernicious downsides of bubbles are obvious: the financial losses and corruption, the wasted efforts and resources, the deep wounds and the scars they leave. Six years after management decided to accept AOL's high-flying stock as currency, Time Warner's shareholders are still bitter and angry at then-CEO Gerald Levin for accepting the deal. Levin, who retreated to Santa Monica to create a high-end holistic mental health clinic, is too blissed out to care. But what about the upside? Hasn't anyone ever made the case for bubbles? Or at least for some bubbles?

•

It seems like a tough case, in part because losses are so easily defined—Mr. Investor buys a hundred shares of Cisco Systems at 70 in 2000. It falls to 18. He's out $5,200. MCI WorldCom's investors saw nearly $180 billion in market capitalization evaporate. But the gains—economic, social, and cultural—are less obvious and more difficult to calculate. It is always thus. Economists note—and have proved—that Wal-Mart has made significant contributions to overall productivity, and provides benefits to millions of consumers in the form of lower prices for everything from giant jars of pickles to Garth Brooks CDs. But the mom-and-pop hardware store that closed in the wake of Wal-Mart's arrival, and the American factory that closed because Wal-Mart demanded its products be sourced in China, makes better copy. Just so, the tales of short-term woe experienced by bubble-burned investors, who constitute a minority of the population, frequently overlook the substantial long-term benefits that accrue to everyone, and to the economy at large, in the years after.

And if you take the long view—in this case, a pretty long view—it's possible to detect a pattern that emerges in bubbles and their aftermaths. Especially bubbles that leave behind a new commercial and consumer infrastructure. With apologies to Oliver Stone, these bubbles, for lack of a better word, are good. These bubbles are right; these bubbles work. Thanks to the American penchant for creative destruction and the U.S. bankruptcy system, investors—and the economy at large—tend to get over bubbles quickly. Bourgeois practicality, suppressed during the bubble, resurfaces. The stuff built during infrastructure bubbles—housing and telegraph wire, fiber-optic cable and railroads—doesn't get plowed under when its owners go bankrupt. It gets reused—and quickly—by entrepreneurs with new business plans, lower cost bases, and better capital structures. And when new services and businesses are rolled out over the new infrastructure, entrepreneurs can tap into the legions of users who were coaxed into the market during the bubble. This dynamic is precisely what has made Google the "it" company of this decade. Solar-powered, Prius-driving, earnings-guidance-refusing, don't-be-evil Google, a company that like so many others was built on the wreckage of Global Crossing and eToys.

Looking back, many similarly iconic companies and industries that have stimulated economic growth, and that helped define America's commercial culture, were either formed in those hothouse bubble environments or can trace their origins to their aftermaths. Consumer packaged goods and mass retailing, data services and mass media, the vast financial services sector, tourism, telecom, and what venture capitalists still call "the Internet space." Sears, the Associated Press, Western Union, Fidelity Investments, Google—they may all have developed anyway. But they certainly would not have developed *as they did* without the Pop! dynamic.

- Between 1846 and 1852, the number of telegraph miles in the United States rose more than tenfold, from 2,000 to 23,000. Excess capacity caused prices to plummet, and most telegraph companies, mainly backed by small local investors, wilted. Within a decade, most lines ended up in the hands of a single consolidator, Western Union. The country wound up with a utility that businesses of all sizes could use. And the rapid spread of cheap telegraphy set other key industrial innovations into motion: the creation of the Associated Press and a quantum leap in news gathering, national markets in stocks, commodities, and business information.

- The investment mania surrounding railroads created a commercial platform that midwifed a national market for goods and services. A spasm of overbuilding in the 1880s spawned vicious rate wars. By 1893, nearly 25 percent of the railroad miles in the United States were in bankruptcy. This time, bondholders—many of them foreigners—were the losers. The winners: J. P. Morgan and other consolidators, as seven large groups wound up controlling about two-thirds of the nation's rail system by the early twentieth century. Consumers and businesses won, too. Many of the industries and companies that would define the twentieth century were built over cheap, far-reaching rail freight systems: Montgomery Ward and Sears, Roebuck, the transport of refrigerated food, and national brands of packaged goods.

- The 1929 stock market crash helped plunge the U.S. economy into a deep depression and scared off an entire generation of investors. The Dow Jones Industrial Average wouldn't regain its 1929 peak until 1954. But in contrast to the other Pop! episodes, the importance of the investment and credit bubble of the late 1920s—and the long-term advantage it created—lay almost wholly in the response it stimulated. As part of the New Deal, the Roosevelt administration and Congress created a new financial infrastructure for the nation: the FDIC (Federal Deposit Insurance Corporation), which made it safe for people to bank again; the Securities and Exchange Commission, which made it safe for people to invest again; and the Investment Company Act, which laid the foundation for the modern asset management business. Such innovations helped bring into being the nation's capital-intensive, credit-driven economy and paved the way for America's global financial dominance in the second half of the twentieth century.

- During the coincident, mutually reinforcing dot-com and fiber-optic bubbles of the 1990s, companies plowed some $30 billion into the ground, building 90 million miles of fiber-optic cable. In 2001, it was estimated that just 5 percent of the fiber-optic capacity was being used. Consumer-oriented firms, from Amazon.com to Webvan, likewise squandered billions of venture capital and public money on breakneck expansion plans. In the end, however, they wired the nation, and brought millions of people into the new medium. In 2006 some 84 million Americans, 42 percent of households, had broadband access at home, according to Nielsen/NetRatings. The list of companies built on this platform includes Vonage and Skype, Google, eBay, and Infosys.

• With the aid of Federal Reserve chairman Alan Greenspan, the U.S. economy cycled almost directly from the dot-com mania into a real estate and housing credit bubble. All the signs are there: the departure from historic trends, the parabolic charts, the invest-at-all-costs mentality, the easy dismissal of sober-minded analysts like Yale economist Robert Shiller, who warned of a real estate bubble in his book *Irrational Exuberance*. In 2004, 23 percent of homes were bought for investment purposes, according to the National Association of Realtors, and 26 percent of mortgages in the first half of 2006 were interest-only mortgages. It's too soon to make any conclusions about the long-term impact of this infrastructure bubble. But so far its salutary effects include the creation of a huge number of jobs and the inflow of investment into long-neglected urban areas.

- F. Scott Fitzgerald wrote that there are no second acts in American life. But as venture capitalist John Doerr noted in October 2006, "There are plenty of second acts in American business." Indeed, many of the same folks who brought us the fiber-optic and dot-com bubble of the 1990s have returned for an encore. Bill Gross, the visionary behind Internet incubator Idealab (PETsMART. com, eToys, Free-PC), has transformed seamlessly into an alternative energy Barnum. In 2001, he founded Energy Innovations, a suddenly hot firm that builds commercial solar energy grids. Vinod Khosla, the former partner at venture-capital power Kleiner, Perkins (Excite@Home), is now an ethanol evangelist. The language emanating from Silicon Valley is eerily familiar. Alternative energy start-ups can change the world, reduce global warming, free America from its ties with tyrannical Middle Eastern regimes, combat inflation, and save the planet—all while making investors rich beyond belief. As they say in the blogosphere: developing.

What to make of this uniquely American cycle of bubbles and innovation? Of course, bubbles are not uniquely American. There was the tulip bubble in Holland in the seventeenth century, and the South Sea bubble in Britain in the early eighteenth century, in which entrepreneurs created new companies and sold stock based on little more than a one-sentence plan. "The most famous of the legendary bubble companies," Edward Chancellor wrote in his chronicle of speculation, *Devil Take the Hindmost*, "was that 'for carrying on an undertaking of great advantage but no one to know what it is.' " (In other words, a hedge fund.) But in general, the rollouts of new technologies in other developed economies have proceeded at a slower and more orderly pace than in the United States, and as a result they have created far less collateral economic activity and spurred less innovation. Because European governments tended to get involved in the rollout of new technologies like the telegraph and the Internet at an earlier stage, they forestalled the types of bubbles that developed in the United States. And it's obvious that the United States has dealt with and processed economic failure more efficiently and effectively than Europe, in part by creating new infrastructure. In the 1930s, the United States responded to the depression by creating the New Deal; Germany responded by creating a fascist regime that set the world on fire.

The Pop! dynamic, in other words, is another brief in the case for American Exceptionalism, the notion that the United States has traced a unique path of social, economic, political and cultural development. A doctrine now fashionable on the right, modern American exceptionalism started in the center, with the 1955 book *The Liberal Tradition in America*, by Harvard political scientist Louis Hartz. The United States wasn't plagued by the socialism, fascism, or violent revolutions that ravaged the Old World, Hartz argued, precisely because it had no history of feudalism against which the masses could revolt.

The assertion that the United States has followed a unique path of historical economic development isn't particularly controversial. Michael Milken noted in the *Wall Street Journal* that "China and India combined to produce nearly half the world's economic output in 1820 compared to just 1.8 percent for the U.S." Today, the United States, with about 4 percent of the world's population, accounts for about one-quarter of the globe's output. And each year, it adds about $308 billion in gross domestic product, an amount roughly equal to the economy of South Korea. No economy has matched the combination of stability, growth, and scale that the United States has shown for the last 150 years. And no economy has demonstrated the ability to post sustained, consistent growth off such a gigantic base.

Is it possible that investment bubbles—particularly those that result in the creation of new national commercial and consumer infrastructures—have proven to be a competitive advantage for the U.S. economy?

Clearly, the way in which Americans rush headlong into investment bubbles, process their failure, and get started on the next one is exceptional. In *The Hypomanic Edge*, psychologist John Gartner argues that the neurotic penchant for jumping off financial cliffs—and then walking away—is part of the American character. Over the centuries, immigrants constituted a self-selecting group of people with short attention spans, tendencies toward enthusiasm, an inflated sense of their own capabilities, and a high level of resiliency—all crucial character traits for entrepreneurs. Who else would get on a leaky boat to endure the passage across the Atlantic for an unknown future? This argument is what I call the Officer Krupke theory of economic growth: we're not deprived on account of we're depraved.

It's tempting to view bubbles as episodic outbursts of American entrepreneurial id. But there's more to the story than national character. Bubbles can form only under certain conditions. Somebody has to provide the soap and the water and the equipment that allows them to be mixed in proper proportion. Character, emotions, and individuals matter. But so do structure, laws, and systems. And the Pop! dynamic could not have played out were it not for

America's unique legal, regulatory, and political infrastructure.

The assumption among economic and business historians is that government action *follows* periods of exuberant private-sector behavior. Carlota Perez, the Venezuelan economist who wrote *Technological Revolutions and Financial Capital: The Dynamics of Bubbles and Golden Ages*, argues that technological revolutions are ultimately "recognized as a threat to the established way of doing things in firms, institutions and society at large," and thus inspire government reaction. Debora Spar, the Harvard historian who proposed a schematic view of innovation in her 2001 book, *Ruling the Waves*, argued that the government sets rules only after a period of entrepreneurial chaos. They're half right.

Because the United States is seen as a free-market nirvana, the role government has played in contributing to the creation of bubbles, piercing or ending them, and helping the economy recover from them, is frequently overlooked. In fact—and this is the second assumption that animates this book—government, through tax credits and patent policies, procurement and legislation, the tax code and direct subsidies, has helped foment, incubate, kick off, and sustain these booms. Congress commissioned Samuel Morse's first telegraph line and granted massive tracts of federal lands to railroad builders. During the Depression, the Roosevelt administration created a new financial infrastructure. The 1996 Telecommunications Act helped spur the fiber-optic blowout, and the housing bubble would have been impossible without Federal Reserve chairman Alan Greenspan, the government-sponsored enterprise Fannie Mae, and the mortgage interest deduction. The alternative energy business—a boomlet well on the way to the bubble—is a harmonic convergence of subsidies, tax credits, and half-baked industrial policy. Meanwhile, the American legal and regulatory infrastructure—the bankruptcy code, the securities regulation regime—allows the economy to process the creative destruction created by investment booms and busts.

Before we proceed, a few words of disclosure. I'm neither an academic economist nor academic historian by profession. This is not an exhaustive study of every bubble that has taken place in the New World since the armor-clad conquistadors arrived in the late fifteenth century. I won't be covering the land speculation of the late eighteenth century, the Florida real estate bubble post–World War I, or the still-unfathomable Ricky Martin bubble of 1999. The rollout of the telephone or the craze for starting auto companies, while important episodes, didn't inspire the amount of volatility and lunacy I look for in bubbles. This isn't a unified theory of investor behavior or efficient markets or a comprehensive investigation into asset price changes over time. Rather, it's an argument based on historical research, reporting, and up-close observation.

And this is not to say that all bubbles are good for the economy (book titles and subtitles always lapse into hyperbole). To repeat, they're useful only when they leave behind a commercial infrastructure that others can use. Still, I believe that seeking the upside of bubbles can shed some light on the cycle of entrepreneurship and capital formation that has distinguished this country's development. If we're casting about for a reason as to how the United States has built itself essentially from nothing to become, for all its faults and failings, the most powerful and prosperous nation in the history of mankind, we have to at least entertain the possibility that bubbles might have played a positive role. And if that's true, then maybe all us chumps who bought Cisco at $70, or used the words "interactive commerce space" in conversation, or who took out an interest-only negative amortization mortgage to buy that fourth preconstruction condo in Miami, have done our part to make America's economy the envy of the world. A final bonus: the bitter experience does yield some lessons as to how people can profit from the madness of the crowds, or at least avoid getting hurt as badly as the doofus next door who bought WorldCom at the top and then bought it again on the dip.

Is all of this a misguided effort to find nobility in our gullibility and greed? Vision in naïveté? Virtue in venality? Wisdom in collective ignorance?

I report, you decide.

2

THE TELEGRAPH

I n his excellent eponymous 1998 book, Tom Standage dubbed the telegraph the Victorian Internet, which earned my nomination for Most Apt Metaphor of the Decade. The concatenation of cable, poles, wires, and electromagnets constructed in the mid-nineteenth century was indeed the original neural commercial network. And the telegraph stands as the first great example of the American Pop! dynamic. In the 1840s, the private sector, with a substantial assist from the federal government, was stricken with telegraph fever. While the European rollout proceeded at a stately, Loire-like pace, the telegraph burst onto the American scene like the furious waves cascading over Niagara Falls. The volatile, frenzied, and disorderly process produced an enormously powerful platform for businesses and industries. And this new commercial infrastructure proved a competitive advantage for a still-young nation, rich in human capital but short of financial capital.

Construction on the first telegraph systems—cumbersome optical systems relying on paddles, mirrors, and relay towers—was backed by European governments as early as the 1790s. After the discovery of electromagnetism in 1820, tinkerers began to toy with efforts to send signals through wires at the speed of light. Enter Samuel F. B. Morse, the Al Gore of the Victorian Internet. A brokenhearted polymath,

Morse was by turns a commercial-minded painter, a Nativist candidate for mayor of New York, a New York University professor, and a would-be government contractor. In February 1825, while in Washington executing a portrait of a foreigner—the Marquis de Lafayette—Morse's wife, Lucretia, died in New Haven. Morse didn't learn the horrible news in time to make the funeral, and the crushing loss spurred him to think about how people could transmit information more quickly.

In the 1830s, Morse was an expatriate painter, although he was more an aspiring Thomas Kinkade than a starving artist. He created *The Gallery of the Louvre*, in which he reproduced thirty-eight of the Paris museum's great masterpieces in miniature. (Morse planned to charge culture-starved Americans to see it.) On a long transatlantic journey in 1832, he and a fellow passenger, Dr. Charles Jackson, fell to talking about electromagnetism. Back in New York, he devised the Morse code, figured out a way to record the signals, and, as artists and academics are wont to do, started agitating for government grants.

In December 1842, Morse strung up wires between two committee rooms on Capitol Hill to demonstrate his technology. But the solons weren't easily fooled. Representative Cave Johnson of Tennessee knew a humbug when he saw it. Congress might just as well start funding research into mesmerism as the telegraph, he said. Nonetheless, in March 1843, Congress passed, by a slim margin (89–83, with 70 abstaining), a bill that appropriated $30,000 "for testing the capacity and usefulness of the system of electro magnetic telegraphs invented by Samuel F. B. Morse of New York, for the use of the Government of the United States." Two years later, Representative Johnson, who had failed to grasp the opportunity to create a new nationwide communications infrastructure, was, naturally, put in charge of the nation's communications infrastructure. In 1845, he was named postmaster general. That would be equivalent to putting an ancient, out-of-it senator from Alaska, like Ted Stevens, who thinks the Internet is "a bunch of tubes," in charge of the Senate committee that oversees the Internet.

Armed with taxpayer funds, Morse built a forty-mile line from Washington to Baltimore, assisted by his contractor, F. O. J. Smith, a former congressman from Maine; Ezra Cornell, a plow salesman from upstate New York; and Alfred Vail, a machinist. The line's first major test came on May 1, when Vail relayed the news that the Whig Party, meeting in Baltimore, had nominated Henry Clay for president, beating the train-carried version of the same news by more than an hour. On May 24, 1844, the first message on the completed line was sent from the Supreme Court to Baltimore: "What hath God wrought?" (It was closely followed by the second dispatch: "Pray tell, are the soft-shell crabs in season?")

What followed was a bizarre tango, in which Morse repeatedly begged Congress to take control of the telegraph or make the extension of the lines a national project, or, failing that, pay him to continue building. For the inventor believed the telegraph was too powerful and important (and too capital-intensive) to leave to the private sector. After all, the United States lacked the financial infrastructure—banks, big insurance companies, financiers—to fund large-scale development. But Congress simply preferred not to. Having provided the seed capital, Congress passed on a second round. Instead, in 1845, the government agreed to lease the original line to the newly formed Magnetic Telegraph Company, a venture backed by Morse, Smith, and former postmaster general Amos Kendall.

The Magnetic Telegraph Company, which wanted to build a large system with New York at its hub, had difficulty raising capital, in part because the revenues on the nation's only commercial telegraph line were less than impressive. In the first four days of April 1845, the Washington office of the Baltimore–Washington, D.C., line brought in precisely one half of one cent. In its first six months of operation, the company notched revenues of $413 and expenses of $3,284. What's more, the government, with Cave Johnson now installed as postmaster general, had imposed a t-mail tax: a tariff of one cent for every four characters sent over the line.

And so the Magnetic's line had to be built in pieces, with capital subscriptions from local investors raised for each segment. Rounding up cash from dry goods merchants and bankers and farmers and tradesmen turned out to be an easier task than wringing it out of Congress. And it's easy to see why. In the 1840s, data moved only as fast as humans could travel, which was very slow indeed. The prospect of transforming business orders, letters, greetings, gossip—in other words, data—into electric impulses, dashes and dots that sped through wires instantaneously, as if by magic, inspired backers. Amos Kendall raised $15,000 from a dozen-odd investors to link New York and Philadelphia, and the line opened in January 1846. By mid-1846, Washington was connected to New York—almost. Since the wires couldn't span the Hudson River, telegraph messages were zapped to Fort Lee, New Jersey, carried across the Hudson by ferry, toted up to a telegraph station in Washington Heights, and then transmitted down to lower Manhattan. Among the first users were speculators—stock brokers eager to get early access to quotes on securities traded in both Philadelphia and New York.

Within a matter of months, the nation was seized by telegraph fever. And not for the first time, an exciting new technology attracted some entrepreneurs who were, well, a little nuts. Manic, undeterred by failure, heedless of practicalities, eager to spend other people's money, armed with unrealistic forecasts, they threw up wires on poles the way kids spray Silly String at birthday parties, fell flat on their face, and built again. Historian Robert Luther Thompson called the period between 1847 and 1852 "methodless en-thusiasm." None proved more methodless or enthusiastic than Henry O'Reilly, the Harold Hill of the early telegraph era. In the fall of 1845, O'Reilly, a charismatic Irish immigrant who had been the postmaster of Rochester, started building a line in Pennsylvania from Lancaster to Harrisburg. This forty-mile line was to be the first link of the grandly named Atlantic & Ohio Telegraph Company. But the pent-up demand for Lancasterites to communicate with their fellow Quaker Staters remained pent up. The first message on the line, on January 8, 1846, read: "Why don't you write, you rascals?" Three months later, the copper wire was dismantled and sold for scrap.

Undaunted by his failure, the congenitally optimistic O'Reilly began building in several directions at once: across upstate New York; throughout the Midwest, from Louisville, Kentucky, south to New Orleans; to the northwest to Chicago; and to St. Louis. Agents, dispatched to towns and cities in between the larger cities to promise riches, sang the virtues of the new communications technology, and separated naive investors from their hard-earned dollars. Sometimes, promoters would promise a town a telegraph station if only the locals would kick in $2,000. Or they would string a wire into town and announce that work could only continue if residents were willing to help fund it. In the classic 1993 *Simpsons'* homage to *The Music Man*, a huckster named Lyle Lanley comes to Springfield and convinces the locals to back the construction of a monorail, leading to this priceless exchange:

Apu: Is there a chance the track could bend?
Lyle Lanley: Not on your life, my Hindu friend.
Barney: What about us brain-dead slobs?
Lyle Lanley: You'll be given cushy jobs.

The telegraph promos didn't quite promise cushy jobs for the brain-dead slobs, but they may as well have. The encomia published by excited local newspapers and O'Reilly's tendency to boosterism created a positive feedback loop.

Due to some strange synapse malfunction, entrepreneurs like O'Reilly believed that in areas lacking sufficient traffic to sustain one telegraph line profitably, the Good Lord would provide sufficient traffic to sustain two or three. A lack of profitable traffic wasn't the only problem. When telegram messages materialized they often couldn't be delivered. Lines failed frequently, and workmanship and expertise was in short supply. Wild animals, floods, and snow knocked out connections. While early adopters paid dearly to use the service, they were frequently disappointed. It was a lot like DSL.

Connectivity was also a major issue. The early telegraph was plagued by constant patent disputes of a type that didn't surface in the government-controlled systems in Europe. In 1847, Morse had licensed his technology to

F. O. J. Smith (to build systems in New England and the old Northwest Territories) and to Amos Kendall (to build systems in the rest of the United States east of the Mississippi). But Royal House, a Vermont inventor, had received a patent on a printing telegraph machine in 1846 and licensed his technology to builders. So did Scottish scientist Alexander Bain. Still others ignored patents and did whatever they damn pleased. As Tom Standage wrote, "Very few of the dozens of telegraph companies that sprang up to meet the explosive demand for telegraphy honored his [Morse's] patent." Like spiteful children, companies using rival patents frequently refused to connect their lines to one another's. So lightning, as the telegraph was known, frequently moved at the shambling pace of a superannuated messenger. In other instances, constant litigation led to injunctions, the seizure of systems, and temporary closures. Here, again, the government played a role. "U.S. courts aggressively defined who held the key telegraph patents and the rights to commercialize them," historian Debora Spar noted. In 1851, when a federal court essentially agreed with Morse that the Bain patents were illegitimate, it was the death knell for the independent Bain systems.

Due to a variety of factors—inefficient systems, too much debt, intense competition, patent struggles—most of the early telegraphs turned out to be terrible investments. The Illinois & Mississippi Telegraph Company, organized in Peoria in 1849, sold 1,000 shares at $50 apiece to small investors. After two years of losses, stockholders were asked to either pay $2.50 per share to hold on, or to sell their stock back to the company at $2.51 per share—a 95 percent haircut. Other companies paid dividends with funds to be used for construction costs. People's Telegraph raised $660,000 by selling shares at $50 apiece so Henry O'Reilly could build a telegraph from Louisville to New Orleans, racing a Kendall-backed line from Washington. When the line went into operation in 1849, O'Reilly rhapsodized:

> *The general prosperity of the lines constructed under the arrangements of the subscriber, in nearly all parts of the United States, and the particular circumstances and location of this line between New Orleans and the North, (traversing the Mississippi Valley and connecting with all the lines constructed by the subscriber elsewhere through the Union), render it needless to dwell even for a moment on the value of this great line between the Gulf of Mexico and the Western and Northern parts of the American Confederacy.*

The next year, the wire was washed away by floodwaters of the Mississippi. The company went bust, and the lines were leased to a new operator for $13,500 per year.

It should be noted that there were a few gentle skeptics of the telegraph in the age of methodless enthusiasm. But they were marginalized figures, easily caricatured as rusticating losers hostile to everything that smacked of modernity. "We are in great haste to construct a magnetic telegraph from Maine to Texas," wrote Henry David Thoreau in *Walden*, published in 1854. "But Maine and Texas, it may be, have nothing important to communicate."

Amid the carnage, the nation got wired quickly. Telegraph wire-miles rose from 40 in 1846 to 2,000 in 1848, and to a whopping 23,283 by 1852, with another 10,000 miles under construction. The Census Bureau proudly noted that "the telegraph system is carried to a greater extent than in any other part of the world and numerous lines are now in full operation for a net-work over the length and breadth of the land." In France, where, as in most of Europe, the government controlled the telegraph's development, there were only 750 miles of wire. Sure, the Europeans had smaller, more rational systems and fewer problems with connectivity and patents. But they also didn't have rate wars.

From the outset, American consumers benefited from the excess capacity, which caused desperate operators to slash prices in an effort to boost volume. In the fall of 1849, three lines, relying on three rival patents, connected New York and Boston. The first was a Morse line, the New York & Boston Magnetic Telegraph Line, which charged fifty cents for ten words or less and three cents per word thereafter. But soon after, the House line (the Boston & New York Printing Telegraph) and the Bain line (New York &

New England Telegraph) opened for business. In the ensuing rate war, the price of telegraphy fell to a penny per word. Good for consumers and businessmen. Bad for investors. The Boston & New York went bankrupt and was eventually taken over by the Associated Press, one of the first lasting businesses built on the new infrastructure.

Indeed, newspapers were one of the first industries to use the telegraph to great effect. At first, the new technology threw the dead tree crowd into a paroxysm of dread (*plus ça change* . . .). James Gordon Bennett, editor of the *New York Herald*, fretted that while magazines might survive, the rapid-fire distribution of information meant "the mere newspapers must submit to destiny and go out of existence." But the telegraph quickly became the newspaperman's friend. Pre-telegraph, news traveled at the speed of sail-powered ships and horses. The only truly fresh news was local news, and foreign coverage was inevitably stale. In May 1846, Bennett, Horace Greeley, and editors from four other newspapers banded together to form the Associated Press. They agreed to work cooperatively on international news and to use their collective buying power to negotiate good deals on telegraph rates. (In some instances, the AP also agreed not to publish disparaging news about telegraph companies.) The telegraph not only made possible a quantum leap in news gathering and in distribution, it paved the way for a new newspaper culture that is still with us today. The AP still provides a significant chunk of news to everyone from the *Washington Post* to Yahoo! Ever mindful of the need to skimp on costs, nineteenth-century newspapers encouraged journalists to telegraph their stories with a shorthand that is still very much in vogue: "POTUS, for president of the United States; yam, for yesterday morning; gx, for great excitement; scotus, for Supreme Court; sfd, for stop for dinner." As in, *YAM, the former POTUS Bill Clinton SFD and ate several quarter-pounders with GX.* (LOL!)

When lines failed, or companies went bankrupt, they weren't just left there like crumbling Roman aqueducts or torn down like homes in the suburbs. They were recapitalized or folded into larger companies with better balance sheets. And by the early 1850s, the stage was set for consolidation. Like the religious revival of the 1820s, it came from upstate New York. Hiram Sibley raised money for a telegraph line in Rochester in 1851 and built a system, the New York and Mississippi Valley Printing Telegraph Company, in part by acquiring beaten-down lines for pennies on the dollar. (He also acquired the House patents.) Ezra Cornell, who had gone into business for himself, was consolidating too. When the New York & Erie Telegraph Company, capitalized at $110,000, failed, he bought it for $7,000 and renamed it the New York & Western Union Telegraph Company. Cornell and Sibley merged their companies in 1856 to form Western Union. Amid the consolidation, ruinous competition continued, despite a short-lived effort to stop the madness. In forming the so-called Treaty of Six

Nations, six large firms agreed to divide traffic and connect with one another. But the treaty brought only a momentary halt to the vicious price and network competition.

During the Civil War years, the telegraph industry— and Western Union in particular—received another significant boost from the federal government. In 1860, Congress passed the Pacific Telegraph Act, under which Hiram Sibley was awarded a contract to build a line from Missouri to San Francisco. Government support came in several forms: $40,000 in cash per year for ten years, and the right to use federal land for rights of way and repair stations. It also fixed prices at $3 for ten words and ensured that the government would be able to use the line. Contending with buffalo and occasionally hostile Native Americans, the Pacific Telegraph Company, which was controlled by Sibley and ultimately merged into Western Union, managed to string the wires to California in just four months. Talk about disintermediation. It instantly made the pony express, which needed more than a week to schlep a letter across the plains, seem pokey. Western Union also enjoyed a symbiotic relationship with the post office. Telegrams could be turned in at post offices, which would forward them to Western Union for transmission. And the post office would deliver messages from Western Union offices.

By the end of the war, in part because it controlled the transcontinental wire, Western Union had become the dominant force in the telegraph industry. In 1866, Sibley used Western Union stock to acquire the company's two largest remaining rivals. When the deals were done, Western Union had 75,686 miles of wire and 2,250 telegraph offices.

A similar dynamic played out with the transatlantic cable, the original global crossing, whose story is ably chronicled by John Steele Gordon in *A Thread Across the Ocean: The Heroic Story of the Transatlantic Cable*. Cyrus Field, a hypomanic entrepreneur born in 1819, rounded up money in May 1854 to start the New York, Newfoundland and London Telegraph Company. When a Brit asked what he would do if the venture failed, "Charge it to profit and loss," said Field. "And go to work to lay another." That's exactly what he did. The first attempt resulted in a loss of $351,000. In October 1856, Field chartered the Atlantic Telegraph Company, and in a few weeks raised 350 shares at £1,000 each.

As with the first above-ground telegraph lines, government assistance proved crucial. A bill signed into law on March 3, 1857, by Franklin Pierce, the day before he left office, gave Field's company a subsidy of up to $70,000 per year. The House of Lords passed similar legislation in July 1857. The cable was paid out off the decks of the USS *Niagara*, the largest ship in the U.S. Navy, and the HMS *Agamemnon*, which were accompanied by naval escorts, courtesy of British and American taxpayers. Despite several false starts, they finally succeeded in completing a functioning cable in August 1858. After the first message came through, a note from Queen Victoria to President James Buchanan, things got a little out of hand. "The triumphant pyrotechnics with which our city fathers celebrated this final and complete subjugation by man of all the powers of nature—space and time included—set City Hall on fire, burned up its cupola and half its roof, and came near destroying the County Clerk's office and unsettling the titles to half the property in the city," wrote New York lawyer George Templeton Strong.

The cable inspired a great deal of globaloney. Cyrus Field's brother, Henry, presaging Tom Friedman's naive kumbayaism of *The Lexus and the Olive Tree*, wrote that it "joins the sundered hemispheres. It unites distant nations, making them feel that they are members of one great family." Three weeks later, the cable went dead, presumably sundering the hemispheres again. And contemporaries thought they had been had. "The cable was soon being referred to as the Great Atlantic Bubble," as telegraph historian Lewis Coe noted. In 1860, Field's company went bust; and he managed to pay creditors just twenty-five cents of each dollar owed. But it wasn't a complete loss. Americans could always figure out some purpose for unused infrastructure. Tiffany & Co. bought pieces of the unused cable, cut them into four-inch pieces, and sold them. (A 4.25-inch segment was on sale in 2006 at the George Glazer Gallery in Manhattan for $600.) Efforts continued after the end of the Civil War, again with government support. Field finally succeeded in laying a lasting cable in 1866. Rates were initially quite exorbitant: $10 a word. Still, between July 28 and October 31, 1867, the cable transmitted 2,772 commercial messages across the Atlantic, bringing in an average of $2,500 a day. Competition came fast and furious: a French company laid a cable in 1869, and rates began to fall. By 1900, there were fifteen threads across the ocean.

The process of wiring the nation continued, but the war was essentially over. A few investors did quite well on the telegraph. Ezra Cornell, the biggest shareholder of Western Union, made enough to start Cornell University. Morse lived out his days in comfort and lived to see a bronze statue of himself unveiled in Central Park. He died on April 2, 1872, at the ripe old age of eighty-one, at 5 West 22nd Street. That year, the telephone, which had its roots in the harmonic telegraph, was on the way in, sowing the seeds of the telegraph's eventual obsolescence.

The economic impact of the telegraph wasn't confined to the jobs its construction created or the value of Western Union's stock. Rather, its impact could be seen in what was built on top of it. The telegraph quickly became a crucial tool for American businesses. Here again, the differences between Europe and America are instructive. Debora Spar writes that in Europe, the telegraph was "a more confined technology, used primarily by big businesses and the state." Britain, the most overtly capitalist European country, followed its more statist neighbors with the Telegraph Acts of 1868 and 1869. The government bought the six main domestic telegraph companies and gave them to the post office to run. The United States briefly considered following the old country's lead. In the 1860s and 1870s, amid complaints of high rates from newspapers, Senator C. C. Washburn of Wisconsin submitted plans under which the government would buy up all existing telegraph lines and put the postmaster general in charge of them. Western Union ultimately beat them back.

No, in the United States, the telegraph was destined to be not an orderly public utility, but a creature of entrepreneurs. Europeans were surprised to learn that Americans used it primarily to send information about business. But they shouldn't have been, for the telegraph was a phenomenally important tool for business. It helped the railroads gain scale and, as Alfred Chandler, the dean of American business historians, notes that it enabled the creation of large-scale industrial operations. But the telegraph had an even broader and deeper impact. The New Economy was more than 120 years in the distant future, but by the time the dust settled on the telegraph investment boom, the U.S. was already transformed into an information economy. With the telegraph, information could be distributed cheaply, shared easily, even traded.

Indeed, the telegraph was the original CrackBerry. "The information supplied by the telegraph was like a drug to businessmen, who swiftly became addicted," Tom Standage wrote. In his 1997 book, *Data Smog*, journalist David Shenk warned of the pernicious effects of all-enveloping information overload. In an 1868 speech, journalist W. E. Dodge warned of the nineteenth-century version of this affliction:

> *The merchant goes home after a day of hard work and excitement to a later dinner, trying amid the family circle to forget business, when he is interrupted by a telegram from London, directing, perhaps, the purchase in San Francisco of 20,000 barrels of flour, and the poor man must dispatch his dinner as hurriedly as possible in order to send off his message to California.*

The hallmark of today's bits-and-bytes economy is the ability to set value free from its geographic confines. And that's precisely what the telegraph did. The telegraph made possible businesses like the credit rating firm Dun & Bradstreet, which traces its origins to 1849. In April 1848, a year in which telegraph connections were spreading throughout the Midwest, the Chicago Board of Trade (CBOT) was founded. In 1865, the nation having been wired, the CBOT introduced standardized futures contracts for trading grain. And with the advent of the transatlantic cable the following year, that market became an international one. Within two weeks after the cable had opened for business, *Harper's Weekly* reported that "the monetary quotations in this city [New York] and London are becoming equalized." The CBOT, which was acquired in 2006 for $8 billion, made Chicago then, as now, a capital of risk trading. And it's no coincidence that stock brokerages were known as "wire houses" until well into the twentieth century. In 1864, J. P. Morgan, based in New York, began working closely with his banker father, Junius Morgan, who was based in London. With the Concorde still more than a century in the future, the telegraph served as a crucial lifeline for those who wished to conduct intercontinental business.

Like Daisy Buchanan, the telegraph had a voice that sounded like money. It led other people to dream and to organize new businesses that would take advantage of this infrastructure. In 1867, E. A. Calahan, annoyed by the boisterous messenger boys running back and forth with stock quotes in his Wall Street office, used telegraph technology to invent the first stock ticker. S. S. Laws, president of the Gold Exchange, developed a ticker as well, and formed the Gold Indicator Company. Now stock and gold quotes, instead of being delivered by hand or limited to those within earshot, were available in something approximating real time. In 1869, Thomas Edison, an itinerant telegraph operator, came to work for Laws. Sleeping in the back room of the Gold Indicator Company, Edison led the typical life of a programmer, subsisting on the nineteenth-century equivalent of Red Bull and Twinkies—"a frugal diet of apple pie washed down with vast amounts of coffee." The $40,000 Edison received for developing his own stock ticker enabled him to set up his own shop. The rest is history. Steel magnate Andrew Carnegie also got his start as a telegraph operator. So did David Sarnoff, the founder of RCA.

Aside from serving as a medium through which the price of money was transmitted, the telegraph became a medium through which money itself could be transmitted. In 1871, in the first example of an electronic funds transfer, Western Union offered customers the opportunity to send money by wire. Using codes and passwords, the service was a sort of latter-day hawala. For those who didn't wish to travel with cash, or who were not sufficiently wealthy to have correspondent relationships with banks, or who just needed cash in a pinch, Western Union was a godsend. Wire transfers have proved to be an extraordinarily durable business. In the fall of 2006, Western Union was spun off as an independent public company by its parent, First Data. The company, which does the same thing Western Union did in 1871, enjoys a 15 percent market share and 30 percent operating margins. In November 2006, Western Union sported a $16.8 billion market capitalization. Not bad for a 135-year-old business model. The money transfer business is hot, in large part because of Latin American immigrants and migrants use the wires to send cash home.

Clearly, the telegraph was not an unalloyed good. The telegraph became a great enabler of financial speculators (among them Cyrus Field, who lost about $6 million on stocks later in life, a victim of the world he made) and hence a contributor to volatility. Like the Internet, the telegraph gave people a sense that they could have more knowledge than they could actually possess. "It is the nervous system of the commercial system," William Orton, president of Western Union, the networking company of the new economy, boasted in 1870. "If you will sit down with me at my office for twenty minutes I will show you what the condition of business is at any given time in any locality in the United States." In a similar vein, *Forbes* in 2002 dubbed sales-management software titan Tom Siebel "the man who sees around corners" because his firm was wired, in real time, to the spending decisions of corporate America. Soon after, Siebel's company, which failed to foresee a slowdown, took a hard fall and became takeover bait for Oracle.

The telegraph didn't lick the business cycle any more than the Internet did. But in the end, it achieved the same amazing feat. The telegraph lashed together the world's commercial centers. It plugged farmers in Nebraska, dry goods merchants in Florida, entrepreneurs in Michigan, speculators in New York, and bankers in London into the same neuro-financial grid. It provided a platform for entrepreneurs to build new businesses and for managers to gain scale and scope. Most important, it led to the creation of national and international financial markets. And so when the next period of government-assisted irrationally exuberant infrastructure investment came, the money didn't have to be raised in small sums from gullible Midwestern burghers. It could be raised in large gulps from gullible Dutch, American, German, and English bankers.

3

THE RAILROADS

Right from the beginning, there were similarities—and synergies—between the development of the railroad and the telegraph. Like the telegraph, the steam railroad was a European import that was put to much greater commercial effect in the New World. Morse's first telegraph line ran alongside the first American railroad, the Baltimore & Ohio. Ground was broken on the B&O on July 4, 1828, by Charles Carroll, ninety years young, the only living signer of the Declaration of Independence. And the two new technologies grew up together. As Alfred Chandler wrote, "the railroad provided the right of way for the telegraph, and the telegraph became a critical instrument in assuring safe, rapid and efficient movement of trains."

But the railroad's Pop! saga unfolded over a longer time frame. For the telegraph, the great period of excess investment, boom, and bust was completed by the 1860s—just when it was getting under way for the railroad. The three decades after the Civil War saw a massive boom in coast-to-coast rail transit, an "orgy of railroad construction" that "infected every region of the country," in the words of historian Maury Klein. The blowout came in the 1880s, a decade in which the United States enjoyed a long economic expansion and elected as president a Democratic governor around whom sexual rumors swirled. Chaotic and frenzied, the railroad boom spawned excess capacity, overnight fortunes, vicious rate wars, financial shenanigans, and falling prices. It was like the telegraph but with much bigger sums of money. Or like the fiber-optic boom, except with handlebar mustaches.

The advent of pervasive, cheap railroad would have a far greater impact on the economy than the advent of pervasive, cheap telegraph. The telegraph offered a quantum leap in data transmission. But for the nineteenth-century U.S. economy, based largely on agriculture and natural resources, a quantum leap in the transmission of *goods* would prove to be far more important. In a huge, sprawling nation, cleaved by deep valleys, high mountains, and wide rivers, the cost and time involved in carting people and things was an impediment to national economic integration. In the 1840s, sending material from Chicago to Philadelphia meant enduring a three-week journey on horse-drawn wagons and river and canal barges. Because of such challenges, the young nation was still a comparative economic weakling. In 1860, the United States produced only 7 percent of the globe's economic output, compared with 20 percent for Great Britain. But the creation of competing weatherproof, 24/7, far-reaching rail systems in the last few decades of the nineteenth century helped forge a golden age for entrepreneurs and companies whose business models depended on transport. Investors in the railroads were frequently left poorer for their troubles, but the entire population grew richer as a result of the enormously powerful new commercial and consumer platform built over the iron rails.

Another triumph of entrepreneurialism, American style? Yes, and no. Just as with the telegraph, merchants and local businesspeople teamed up to build the first small local railroads—with government help. Indeed, in the first phase of railroad expansion, between 1830 and 1860, states fell over themselves to offer aid and comfort to railroads. The construction of the B&O, which reached Harper's Ferry, West Virginia in 1834, was supported by the State of Maryland. Promoters raised $2 million in stock to build the Boston & Worcester, which was extended to reach Albany in 1841. But the Commonwealth of Massachusetts contributed $1 million in stock and lent $4 million to the company. Ohio granted property tax exemptions for all railroads through 1852. Georgia built the Western & Atlantic Railroad, which, upon its completion in 1851, linked Atlanta and Chattanooga, Tennessee. Virginia typically bought 60 percent of all shares issued by railroads in the commonwealth. "In the south before the Civil War," historian August Veenendaal wrote in his 2003 book, *American Railroads in the Nineteenth Century*, "more than half of the total construction capital of the railroads came from states or towns." In the 1850s, taxpayers effectively provided about a quarter of the $737 million investment in railroads.

In the mid-nineteenth century, the federal government didn't have much in the way of an army, a central bank, or a tax base—assets it could use to help conjure rail lines into existence. But it did possess one huge resource: land. The federal government got into the railroad business in 1850, when Congress granted land to three states—Illinois, Alabama, and Mississippi—to encourage the construction of a 705-mile line snaking alongside the Mississippi River from Mobile to Chicago. The Illinois Central was completed in 1856, the same year the first railroad bridge spanned Mississippi. Now, offering Americans something of great value for free in the nineteenth century was like offering DVD players to twenty-first-century Christmas shoppers at Wal-Mart for $19.97. The result was a stampede. Between 1850 and 1872—the railroad land-grant years—the federal government deeded what economic historian Robert Fogel dubbed an "empire of land to promoters who promised to build railroads across the west." In all, some 170 million acres of prime (and not-so-prime) government land was apportioned to eighty railroads. Not surprisingly, nearly half of the lines for which land was granted were never built or completed, and about 35 million acres of land were returned, unused. That left private railroad companies holding 131.35 million acres—a swath of American soil equal to the combined acreage of Colorado and Wyoming.

A patchwork of small-scale, linear lines connecting existing population centers began to take shape: 9,000 miles in 1850 and 30,626 by 1860, virtually all of them east of the Mississippi. The system, such as it was, struggled with connectivity. Several factors worked against the construction of the type of rational systems that were being built in Europe under the direction of strong central governments. In Germany, France, and Belgium, for example, the governments paid for railroad construction, planned routes, and dictated rates. In America, since states drove the development process, there was no central planning. And building railroads was far more capital intensive than setting up telegraph service. It required huge amounts of timber (for ties and bridges), iron (for rails), buildings (for storage and maintenance), and labor (for construction and grading). The United States lacked the private capital, and states lacked the public capital to support long-haul lines. As a result, standards were devised on the fly. Many railroads used gauges of different widths, so that cars traveling on one couldn't move seamlessly onto other rails. "By 1861, New York City had three great rail systems which were largely shut off from through connections with lines terminating in rival cities due to different gauges," historians George Taylor and Irene Neu wrote. Many of the Confederate states formally rejoined the United States in 1870, but it wasn't until 1886 that the Confederacy's railroads gave up their peculiar broad-gauge roads and agreed to convert them to standard width.

During the Civil War, when infrastructure construction became an issue of national security, the foundation was laid for large, integrated train systems. The Pacific Railroad Bill, signed July 1, 1862, authorized two private companies to build a line to the Pacific: the Central Pacific was to work east from Sacramento, while the Union Pacific would forge a path west from Omaha. Congress believed the construction of both would help "to secure to the government the use of the same for postal, military and other purposes."

In *Nothing Like It in the World*, his paean to American entrepreneurial pluck, Stephen Ambrose concluded that the continental railroads "could not have been built without the government aid in the form of gifts." And how. The government provided several crucial means of direct support. First, there was the free use of money. For each forty-mile section certified by inspectors, the companies would receive thirty-year U.S. bonds: $16,000 per mile on the plains; $32,000 per mile on the plateaus; and $48,000 per mile in the mountains. The government offered to pay the 6 percent annual interest on the bonds, although after thirty years, the companies were to repay all the interest and the principal. The Pacific Railroad Act of 1864, passed two years later, allowed the firms to collect bonds each time twenty miles of track was certified. Between them, the Union Pacific and the Central Pacific were effectively lent more than $53 million by Congress, with no payments required until the late 1890s. Better long-term deals on cheap money couldn't be found until the Las Vegas condo market in 2004. (The railroads ultimately paid back the loans in 1898 and 1899.)

Second, there was land. The railroads were given land for rights of way: two hundred feet on both sides of the road, as well as land for stations and machine shops. But most importantly, the 1864 act stipulated that for each twenty miles of track, the railroads would receive ten alternate sections of land, adding up to about 12,800 acres per mile, or twenty square miles. The land was crucial for two reasons. The companies could borrow against the land to raise much-needed cash—rail-equity lines of credit! And they could sell the land to generate cash. "The Union Pacific in the 1870s was selling its land to farmers in Nebraska at $3 to $5 an acre," railroad historian John Stover noted. In 1880, the Department of the Interior estimated the total value of the lands granted to the railroads at $391 million.

The extraordinary story of the transcontinental railroad, told in fine detail by Ambrose and in *Union Pacific* by Maury Klein, is a great case study in government procurement via competitive outsourcing. Ground was broken on December 2, 1863. In 1866, Congress passed legislation that essentially allowed the Central Pacific and the Union Pacific to build as fast as they could. According to Ambrose, "the company that won would get the largest share of the land and the biggest share of the bonds," and the cost to the government would be the same. Engaging in Stakhanovite labors, the competing roads pressed their animals, miserable employees, and steam-belching machines to go all out. On May 10, 1869, in a ceremony live-blogged by telegraph, the golden spike was driven in Promontory, Utah, uniting the two lines. But the completed railroad was seen as a beginning, not the end. Leland Stanford, president of the Central Pacific and later a senator from California, proclaimed: "The day is not far distant, when three tracks will be found necessary to accommodate the commerce and travel which will seek a transit across the continent."

Stanford was 100 percent right, and 90 percent wrong. Fueled by land grants, a lattice of rails, trestles, and bridges was quickly laid across the plains. In the south, the Atchison, Topeka and Santa Fe Railway got started with a 3-million-acre land grant in 1863. In 1870, construction started on the Northern Pacific Railway, which aimed to connect Lake Superior to the Pacific Northwest. Endowed with 44 million acres of land grants and capitalized at $100 million, it managed to complete only five hundred miles before falling into receivership in 1873—which is probably why Johnny Mercer didn't write a song about it, as he did with the Atchison. Financier Henry Villard snapped up the carcass for $8 million and finished it in 1883. Also in 1883 came the Southern Pacific Railroad, linking Los Angeles to Texas. Later still, James J. Hill built the Great Northern Railway, which skirted the border from Duluth to Seattle.

Between 1865 and 1873, spurred by western development, rail mileage in the United States doubled.

It's easy to see why businessmen were so enthused about long-haul roads. These threads across the continents were truly transformative. In 1860, writes Maury Klein, to move 18,000 tons of freight across the plains required 12,000 men, 8,000 mules, 68,000 oxen, and 6,900 wagons. It took a stage coach thirty days to cover the 2,189 miles from St. Louis to San Francisco. By boat, the same journey would take thirty-five days—and you'd have to schlep across the Isthmus of Panama. With the iron horse hauling people and goods across the plains at speeds of up to 60 miles per hour, the expense, discomfort, and time inherent in such treks was reduced dramatically.

So it's no surprise that railroad exuberance began to spill over into popular culture. "Abroad and at home it has equally nationalized people and cosmopolized nations," an anonymous scribe wrote in 1867 in the *North American Review*. "Increased communication, increased activity, and increased facilities of trade destroy local interests, local dialects, and local jealousies. . . . Thoughts are quickly exchanged, and act upon each other. Nations can no longer, except willfully, persist in national blunders . . . The same problems perplex at once the whole world, and from every quarter light floods in upon their solution."

The Union Pacific sent the excitable, pastoral Walt

Whitman into a spasm of rapture. In *Leaves of Grass* (1871), he wrote:

> *I see over my own continent the Pacific Railroad, sur-*
> *mounting every barrier;*
> *I see continual trains of cars winding along the Platte,*
> *carrying freight and passengers;*
> *I hear the locomotives rushing and roaring, and the*
> *shrill steam-whistle,*
> *I hear the echoes reverberate through the grandest*
> *scenery in the world;*
> *I cross the Laramie plains—I note the rocks in gro-*
> *tesque shapes, the buttes;*
> *I see the plentiful larkspur and wild onions—the bar-*
> *ren, colorless, sage-deserts;*
> *I see in glimpses afar, or towering immediately above*
> *me, the great mountains—I see the Wind river and*
> *the Wahsatch mountains;*
> *I see the Monument mountain and the Eagle's Nest—I*
> *pass the Promontory—I ascend the Nevadas . . .*

Alas, as investments, some of these roads were barbaric yawps. Western railroads were built through largely vacant land, seeking to create demand and American settlement rather than to serve it. "The whole country is opening up, all we want is capital to develop it," Mark Twain and

Charles Dudley Warner wrote in their 1873 novel, *The Gilded Age*. "Slap down the rails and bring the land into market." Sociologist Max Weber put it in more academic terms: "In Europe the railroad system facilitates traffic. In America, it creates it." And it didn't matter to many of the promoters if the traffic didn't materialize quickly. Insiders were furiously lining their pockets through the creation of "construction companies." Insiders at the Union Pacific in 1864 organized the Crédit Mobilier (which is French for proto-Enron). The Union Pacific hired the Crédit Mobilier to build several hundred miles of roads, essentially ripping off public shareholders to enrich a few insiders and their connected friends. As part of an effort to stave off an investigation, Congressman Oakes Ames, who headed the Crédit Mobilier, later doled out shares to other representatives. "In order fully to appreciate construction company practices in the early days," Harvard economist William Z. Ripley wrote, "one must imagine a company of promoters not only devoid of capital but without any considerable assets in the way of character."

The railroad construction boom had collateral effects far beyond the Crédit Mobilier. The government regarded the Union Pacific and Central Pacific as industrial policy, decreeing that the rails used be made in the United States. Between 1870 and 1880, more than 80 percent of all steel production fed the voracious rail industry. As they sucked up ever-growing quantities of coal, timber, iron, and steel, the railroads stimulated the creation of huge businesses and fortunes. The rising demand spurred companies to innovate, to invest, and to turn what had previously been small-scale industries into profitable behemoths. None did it better than Andrew Carnegie, the former telegraph operator and railroad investor who set up a steel company in the late 1870s, and through the relentless pursuit of efficiency forged a huge company. In Carnegie's case, the fortune built by the railroads' commodity supplier would prove greater and longer-lasting than virtually all the fortunes amassed by railroad owners and users, save that of John D. Rockefeller.

The post-Civil War railroad boom also stimulated another long-lasting industry that would come to define the twentieth century: Wall Street. Railroads had a constant thirst for capital, and much of it came in the form of stocks and bonds sold by U.S. bankers to investors in France, England, Germany, and the Netherlands. In 1890, about one-third of railroad securities were held by foreigners. Between 1865 and 1900, Europeans bought about $2.5 billion in American securities. Virtually all of them were railroad stocks and bonds; there wasn't much else traded on the New York Stock Exchange. As Thomas Kessner notes in *Capital City*, the growth of the railroads helped New York cement the position it still holds today: the nation's financial center. "Its stock and bond markets dominated the trade in securities; its banks held most of the nation's cash reserves, and its investors controlled the massive new railroad corporations." J. P. Morgan, who would dominate Wall Street for the first portion of its modern era, came of age as a railroad banker. His first big coup came in 1879, when he helped William Vanderbilt, the son of railroad mogul Cornelius Vanderbilt, sell 250,000 shares of New York Central stock. In the 1880s, Morgan began selling bonds for railroads, placing directors on their boards, and getting involved in bankruptcies when railroads keeled over.

The money raised by Morgan and others was put to work. In the 1880s, some $4 billion of cash was funneled into the creation of 71,000 miles of new railroads, "a figure which was more than the construction of any two preceding decades in railroad history," according to historian John Stover. In the previous fifty years, the three largest countries in Europe didn't lay that much steel. New lines were built all over the place: east, west, north, and south. But many of them were duplicative. By 1885, there were five trunk lines from New York to Chicago, three of which were already near bankruptcy.

Demand was certainly rising. Passenger miles per year rose from about 5 billion in 1870 to 12 billion in 1890. In 1890, railroads hauled 79.2 billion ton miles of freight and employed 750,000 people. Robert Fogel notes that whereas in 1851, boats carried six times as much freight as railroads, in 1889–1890, railroads carried five times as much freight as boats. The railroads were real businesses with real revenues. But they didn't merit the valuations they received. While the industry's total capitalization quadrupled from $2.5 billion in 1870 to $10 billion in 1890, the industry's revenues rose by a much smaller amount, from $400 million to $1 billion.

These weren't price-to-earnings ratio overvaluations such as were seen with Amazon.com in the fall of 2000. But for the time, the P/Es were clearly out of whack. Railroads were burdened with high fixed costs like maintenance, debt repayment, and coal, which ate up about two-thirds of revenues. And when high fixed costs are tossed in a shaker with excess capacity, they form a lethal cocktail. For railroads in the 1880s, life was like contemporary electoral politics: a permanent state of war. Rate wars were a constant feature of the business. Faltering lines, which desperately needed cash to keep current on debt payments, usually picked the fights, which was a little like a scrawny kicker getting in the face of a defensive end. The death spiral continued even after companies fell into bankruptcy: freed from paying their interest costs, they could afford to keep cutting prices.

Jay Gould, a compulsive speculator and relentless buyer and seller of railroads, was one of the biggest forces in the price wars. But there were plenty of other mischief makers. New redundant roads were built solely for the purpose of being sold to competitors. The New York, Chicago and St. Louis Railroad was built in 1881 by George I. Seney and

Calvin Brice to mimic William Vanderbilt's Lake Shore & Michigan Southern Railway and Gould's Wabash, St. Louis and Pacific Railway. In 1882, Vanderbilt bought it.

There were forces of order. In July 1885, as Vanderbilt, backed by Andrew Carnegie and John D. Rockefeller, was building a line in southern Pennsylvania simply to spite George Roberts of the Pennsylvania Railroad, J. P. Morgan invited the protagonists on his boat, the *Corsair*, and kept them cruising around New York Harbor until they ironed out a deal—and agreed to pay him a hefty fee. And just as the big telegraph companies did with the Treaty of Six Nations, the railroads formed pools to set rates and divide traffic among themselves. But consumers complained loudly and sought relief from state legislatures. And these pools were shark infested. Early in 1886, the Atchison blew up the Transcontinental Association, which tried to fix rates going across the plains, by unilaterally cutting rates. The members of the pool quickly went medieval on one another. Within a month, freight and passenger rates fell by 75 percent.

Such arrangements, doomed from the outset, were rendered moot in 1887 with the passage of the Interstate Commerce Act. The first big piece of federal regulation surrounding railroads forced them to disclose rates to the public and created the Interstate Commerce Commission, which was empowered to investigate railroads. In fact, the whole notion of pools was comically out of step with the prevailing business ethos and logic of the day. The bloody competition was a boon to Americans—and a competitive advantage. In Europe, it was a different story. As with the telegraph, the rollout of railroads was more sedate. Between 1860 and 1880, when U.S. rail miles tripled, the figure in Great Britain rose by only about 60 percent. As with the telegraph, there wasn't much reckless competition and overbuilding in Europe. And the consumer clearly was not king. "In Britain and Germany such [pooling] arrangements were wholly acceptable," wrote Alfred Chandler. "Only in the United States did the protests of shippers, expressed in terms of antimonopoly values, result in legislation to guarantee continuous competition between companies serving the same regions."

As U.S. railroads slugged it out like desperate contenders on an undercard, the cost of freight fell sharply. In 1858, shipping a bushel of wheat by rail from Chicago to New York cost 38.61¢; in 1870 it was down to 26.11¢, and in 1890, 14.3¢. The average rate per ton mile of freight fell from $1.93 in 1867 to 94¢ and 84¢ in 1895. Railroads weren't just cheaper, they were faster. By the 1880s, freight moved from Philadelphia to Chicago in two days or less.

All of which was great news to the nineteenth-century version of bandwidth hogs. The combination of increased velocity—a wider, faster pipe—and lower prices was powerful, and a huge spur to innovation. With the railroad becoming increasingly pervasive and increasingly cheap, it made sense for Americans in the nation's largest single sector—agricultural commodities—to start shipping their products over long distances. The first patent for a refrigerator car was issued in 1867. Within a few years, Americans were enjoying fresh strawberries shipped from southern Illinois, bananas shipped from New Orleans, California citrus, Texas beef, and grains and corn from the upper Midwest. By 1890, the increasingly industrial North Atlantic region was importing two-thirds of its beef and more than half its corn. The railroad was the original food network.

As freight got cheaper and railroads continued to extend their reach, shippers started climbing the value chain. The railroad made it possible to acquire commodities in bulk, process them efficiently in a central location, and ship the finished goods to distant points for sale. In 1882, Gustavus Swift began building a national meat-packing and distribution company. He was followed quickly by Armour & Co. and Hormel. Suddenly, a host of branded, processed food products—many of which still fill the aisles of Stop & Shop today—burst onto what had suddenly become a national market: Campbell's Soup and C. W. Post Grape-Nuts, Pillsbury flour and H. J. Heinz ketchup, Aunt Jemima pancake mix and Colgate toothpaste. In the eighteenth century, excess grains farmed in the Midwest were processed and floated downriver to market as whiskey. In the late nineteenth century, excess grains farmed in the Midwest were processed in St. Louis and Milwaukee, and shipped east in refrigerated tanker cars as branded beers: Anheuser-Busch, Schlitz, and Pabst. Time and again, marketers in the last few decades of the nineteenth century were pleasantly surprised at their ability to turn new products into national staples. Ivory, the floating soap developed by Procter & Gamble in 1879, became a national brand within a few years. Coca-Cola, first peddled on a small scale in 1887, was distributed in every state by 1895.

This process of rationalization and standardization, and the widespread use of logistics, all of which were fueled by the telegraph and the railroad, contributed mightily to a fundamental reordering of the U.S. economy. As Maury Klein accurately concluded, "the United States in the late nineteenth century may have been the ideal hothouse for the rapid flowering of a private economy." Formerly a collection of regional economies scattered across a vast space, America was coming together as a single, unitary commercial machine. And just as the massive investment in information technology helped tamp down inflation in the 1990s and the first decade of the twenty-first century, the excess capacity in railroads helped contribute to the sustained and wondrous deflation the economy experienced between 1865 and 1900. Prices fell across the board, and yet the nation prospered and boomed, so that by 1900, the United States would account for 15.8 percent of the world's output.

The economy also busted, in part due to one of the great ironies of the gilded age. For the railroad companies, the giant firms that had done so much to enable rationalization and economies of scale, seemed to willfully ignore the lessons the rails taught managers. As excess capacity grew, railroad barons didn't respond rationally—by simply merging and consolidating, cutting costs, or scaling back ambitions. No, they did the opposite. It was bizarro world. Given the failure of pools, each assumed the way to grab a sufficient amount of traffic was to build or acquire enough rails to build proprietary nationwide systems. And so in the late 1880s, even as they were losing money, railroads were hellbent on expansion. The Atchison's mileage rose 150 percent from 1884 to 1888, much of it in the nation's still-large empty quarter. In 1889, it failed. In the South, the Richmond Terminal Company gained control of more than sixty separate railroad companies and nearly 8,900 miles of track, making it the second largest in the country. Charles Francis Adams, the New England intellectual aristocrat who served as president of the Union Pacific in the 1880s, couldn't comprehend the behavior of his industry counterparts. "Great corporations, one after another, have contracted the madness, and have built hundreds of miles of roads, almost paralleling each other." By 1893, as historian Vincent Carosso reported, there were thirty-three railroad companies capitalized at more than $100 million each.

Together, they controlled about 70 percent of the nation's rail system.

The 1890s resembled the 1990s in more ways than one. Companies that were losing money on operations spent cash on corporate bling. But instead of slapping their names on stadiums and building gleaming glass headquarters, they built luxurious stations and depots. St. Louis's Union Station, built to serve eighteen different railroads, was completed in 1894. To fool shareholders, the railroad companies played financial games. The failing Atchison significantly overstated income by, among other things, treating millions of dollars in rebates and uncollectible balances as assets, and by simply adding to earnings when it suited management. The B&O in 1896 revealed that in a seven-year period it had declared about $6.3 million in dividends while earning only $1 million.

It all came to a quick end in 1893. When an industry is highly indebted, and the prices it charges are falling, and companies have to cheat in order to show profits, it doesn't take much of an economic hiccup to send the whole train steaming over the cliff. A financial panic, touched off by the failure of Barings Bank in London, helped set off a recession in the United States that lasted for nearly four years. Pop! By 1894, 192 railroads representing 41,000 miles of track and a total capitalization of $2.5 billion—about one quarter of the industry—were in receivership, including huge companies like the Northern Pacific, the Baltimore & Ohio, the Reading Company, and the Union Pacific. The railroads, which had stimulated so much demand for labor and manufactured goods, dragged the rest of the economy down when they stopped building, buying, and hiring.

Enter the consolidators: J. P. Morgan; Jacob Schiff of Kuhn, Loeb; and Edward Harriman. Like one of today's vulture funds, Morgan perfected a system for restructuring bankrupt railroads. He would swap existing debt for stock, raise cash to fund new debt and working capital, sell off assets, place trusted partners on the board, and consolidate. Stockholders in many of the smaller railroads ended up with nothing, and bondholders were crammed down. In 1895, only 30 percent of railroad stock was paying dividends. Most of the affected investors were foreigners. Among five of the largest bankrupt railroads, the majority of stock was held by foreigners, "and of course the bond holdings, especially in England, were even heavier in proportion," William Z. Ripley wrote. The end result: by 1906, seven major interest groups controlled nearly two-thirds of the country's railroad mileage, or 138,000 of 224,000 miles.

By the late 1890s, the railroad's investment cycle was essentially over. But the economic impact had just begun. The final years of the nineteenth century saw a wave of mergers that created gigantic companies and trusts—U.S. Steel, General Electric, AT&T. The telegraph and the telephone allowed the growing cadre of professional managers to run such firms. And the railroad—remember, there were no cars or trucks—provided the rapid, reliable, dependable, schedulable transport that afforded the companies the ability to run integrated operations.

But the railroads also served as a crucial platform for small, growing companies and for entirely new industries that took flight in the 1890s. By cutting inventory and freight costs, the railroad paved the way for large-scale retailers. The department stores that began to pop up in urban downtowns, and that would define the nation's consumer culture for the next half century, were creatures of the railroad. In 1876, John Wanamaker opened his first Philadelphia department store, which he dubbed "the Grand Depot," in a former freight building. On opening day, seventy thousand eager shoppers thronged the aisles.

The real innovation came out of Chicago, which by the early 1890s was served by at least thirty freight lines. Cheap rail made it possible for start-up retailers to reimagine their customer base—from the small group of shoppers who lived within a few hours' travel to the much larger group of consumers, 63 million strong, who lived within reach of the post office and the railroad. They could publicize their wares through catalogs, take payment by mail, and beat the prices of local merchants by buying in bulk, saving on overhead, and running efficient operations. Thanks to the railroad, distribution, while a challenge, would not be a barrier.

One of the nation's first mail-order companies, Montgomery Ward, started in 1872 with a one-page list of goods, mostly clothes that were pitched to farmers and shipped by rail. But it quickly evolved into "a department store in print for the farmer," with huge selection and little overhead. It was like Amazon.com. The 240-page 1883 catalog featured 10,000 items. By 1900, when the 1,200-page catalog offered "wholesale prices and truthful descriptions of 70,000 things," the company was shipping thirteen thousand packages a day and racking up sales of about $9 million.

But Montgomery Ward didn't have the field to itself. It didn't even have the Midwest to itself. Richard Warren Sears, a freight agent in Minnesota, began selling watches by mail in 1886, and, with the help of watchmaker Alvah Roebuck, launched a catalog in 1891 (it mostly had watches and jewelry). The catalog grew, and the company began to take off after Julius Rosenwald became involved in the business in 1895. That year, as it furiously shipped out orders generated by its 770-page catalog, the company boasted of "selling four suits every minute, one buggy every 10 minutes, a watch a minute."

In *The Long Tail*, Chris Anderson cites the 1896 Sears catalog as an early example of how retailers can make money selling small numbers of huge numbers of items. True enough. But the Sears catalogs of that era also stand as testimony to the way that excessive investment in railroads made possible an entirely new mode of retailing that was both profitable and enormously satisfying to consumers. Leafing through Sears's 1897 785-page catalog, one encounters an astonishing array of goods: Richardson & Robbins canned plum pudding, California raisins, Russian caviar and Frazer axle grease, Fuller's calf weaners and the Whitney automatic pipe wrench, the Western Star electric washer, windmills and corn shelters, men's baseball shoes and ladies' umbrellas, absurd flowery hats and *Robert's Rules of Order*, gold watches and sterling silver baby bells, zithers and harmonicas, Winchester rifles and fencing foils, bedroom sets and bicycles. On and on it goes. This sort of selection, available to a farmer raising corn in Kansas, wasn't available to Turkish pashas or Queen Victoria. The catalog neatly encapsulates the twentieth-century American commercial culture: national brands serving national markets, vast consumer choice, efficiencies gained by economies of scale, and price competition—all made possible by the exuberant, foolish, mad overinvestment in an early nineteenth-century technology.

4

THE FINANCIAL
NEW DEAL

I t's difficult to think of anything positive that came of the 1929 stock market crash. Sure, the bursting bubble unleashed some entrepreneurial energy—all those apple sellers on the streets of big cities. But the market meltdown and the ensuing long, grisly slide into depression was an unambiguous, searing disaster. In the 1920s, dangerous excess capacity and overinvestment bloomed in stocks, in clandestine gin stills, and, above all, in the fuel for speculation and consumption: credit. A twentieth-century world of finance was hastily erected on a rickety nineteenth-century scaffolding, and it all came crashing down when the bubble popped in the fall of 1929. The importance of the bubble of the 1920s—and the long-term advantage it created for the American economy—didn't lie in the infrastructure created during the Roaring Twenties. Rather, it lay in the response it stimulated.

As part of the New Deal, Franklin Delano Roosevelt and the Democratic Congress created a great deal of valuable long-lasting physical infrastructure: the George Washington Bridge, the Hoover Dam, the Appalachian Trail, to name a few. They also created a valuable lasting new financial infrastructure. The New Deal overhauls of the banking, securities, and home lending industries were bitterly opposed by bankers and their Republican political allies.

But the programs resuscitated the comatose patient. Don't take it from me. Take it from Federal Reserve chairman Ben Bernanke: "Only with the New Deal's rehabilitation of the financial system in 1933–35 did the economy begin its slow emergence from the Great Depression," he wrote. As important, the sturdy New Deal platform would serve as a launching pad for a new culture of credit, lending, asset management, and investing—industries that spurred America to global financial dominance in the second half of the twentieth century.

In the 1920s, conditions were ripe for a boom fueled, finally, by domestic capital. After a recession ended in July 1921, the economy expanded nicely throughout the decade. Business enjoyed a favorable political climate, as laissez-faire Republicans controlled the White House and Congress. With Europe's economic powers having destroyed one another during World War I, New York surpassed London as a financial center. The United States, which had been perpetually starved for capital, became a global creditor. In 1914, the United States owed the rest of the world $3.8 billion; by 1920, the rest of the world owed the United States $12.5 billion. Once again, a hot new communications technology—radio—fueled investor interest and inspired one-worlders. RCA head David Sarnoff, having taken one too many sips of the Kool-Aid, enthused that "Radio may end war, for its mission is to bring the whole world into friendly communication." (Never mind that wireless communication actually made stirring up hate easier and became an effective tool in waging war.) RCA, the iconic and highly volatile stock of the decade, popped from $1\frac{1}{2}$ in 1921 to $77\frac{7}{8}$ in 1925, and peaked at 420 in 1928. Take that, Google!

By any measure, the expansions of the 1920s were impressive. Corporate profits rose more than 80 percent between 1921 and 1928. The Dow Jones Industrial Average more than doubled between the beginning of 1921 and the end of 1925, from 72.67 to 156.66. Individual investors, many of whom had bought Liberty Bonds during World War I, began to open brokerage accounts and take up shares of investment trusts, the era's version of mutual funds. Starting in 1921, when the International Securities Trust of America came to market, investment trusts raised cash from the public and deployed capital as their managers saw fit without much disclosure. In 1926, 160 investment trusts had combined assets of about $1 billion.

More important was the flip side of the ownership society: a debtorship society. The Federal Reserve, the nation's central bank, established in 1913, provided a crucial source of liquidity. By controlling interest rates and lending money to banks, the new government institution quickly assumed a vital role in the nation's economic life. And banks—and pretty much everybody else—started to lend money with something close to abandon. Credit was being extended to consumers to buy durable goods like refrigerators: 630,000 would be sold in 1929, up from 11,000 in 1922. In 1919, General Motors formed the General Motors Acceptance Corp. to finance the growing number of car purchases; its book of loans rose from $25.7 million to $401 million in 1929. Then as now, Florida was the epicenter of land speculation. Backed by loans from banks, insurance companies, investment firms, and savings and loans, everyone from Boston scam artist Charles Ponzi to former secretary of state and evolution foe Williams Jennings Bryan, was subdividing and selling swampland. "The Florida real estate boom was the first indication of the mood of the twenties and the conviction that God intended the American middle class to be rich," John Kenneth Galbraith wrote in *The Great Crash, 1929*. In 1930, economist Charles Persons found that mortgage debt on urban real estate rose from $11.07 billion in 1920 to $27.1 billion in 1929, up 144 percent. "We are urged to install delicate tinted bathrooms on the installment plant," Persons wrote. "We may have oil-burning furnaces on easy payments."

"Everybody I knew was in the bond business, so I supposed it could support one more single man," said Nick Carraway in *The Great Gatsby*, published in 1925. Indeed it could, old sport. Between 1920 and 1928, the amount of corporate bonds and notes outstanding rose from $26.1 billion to $47.1 billion, while the volume of securities issued by state and local public securities nearly tripled, from $11.8 billion to $33.6 billion. In the utility and banking industries, holding companies—a corporate structure in which a small amount of capital could control a huge network of companies through the use of leverage—became the norm.

Banks also began to extend credit to investors to buy stocks on margin. The government supply of cheap money spurred an early form of what is now known on Wall Street as the carry trade. Banks would borrow money from the New York Federal Reserve Bank at 4 or 5 percent and then lend it to brokers or investors to buy stocks at 6 or 8 or 12 percent. Booyah! In 1926, the call market (as it was known) amounted to $2.5 billion. In 1927, the Dow rose by a third. In 1928, when the Dow popped another 50 percent, brokers' loans soared to $5.6 billion. Commercial banks, which had historically avoided the stock business, led the way by establishing securities units. At the end of 1928, National City Bank had deposits of $1.35 billion—and loans to brokers of $225 million. And because the Federal Reserve didn't object, all sorts of nonfinancial corporations joined the wild party. "Thousands of corporations, convinced that stock market yield made it more fruitful to speculate with surplus funds than reinvest, put cash in the call loan market," wrote historian James Olson. The movie studio Warner Bros. set up its own bank. Through 1929, Standard Oil was lending about $70 million to brokers. And there were no signs that those lending against stock took measures to guard against their exposure. Hedging was something that gardeners did.

Why bother to take out insurance against a downturn? In November 1927, President Calvin Coolidge proclaimed that America was "entering upon a new era of prosperity," and economists and analysts began to speak of a New Era of perpetual growth, perpetually rising stocks, and harmony between business, government, and life. "The new faith permeated the churches, the courts, the colleges, the press," Arthur Schlesinger Jr. wrote. "It developed an economics of success and a metaphysics of optimism." In this New Era, stocks were investments for the masses and could be safely bought on margin. Discount brokerage firms like Charles Schwab had yet to appear, but savvy marketers like Charles Mitchell were on the scene. The president of National City Bank, Mitchell mimicked the marketing techniques of chain stores and turned his branches into mini-financial department stores. He used sales contests to incentivize his three-hundred-person sales force to move the most product: annuities, Peruvian bonds, domestic stocks, and investment trusts.

In 1928, things really started to get bubblicious. Analysts extrapolated existing trends and blithely adopted a Manichean view of the link between partisan politics and investing. Roger Babson, an analyst known as the Sage of Wellesley, proclaimed in September 1928 that "if [Democratic nominee New York governor Al] Smith should be elected with a Democratic Congress we are almost certain to have a resulting business depression in 1929." When Smith lost to Herbert Hoover and Republicans retained control of Congress, it inspired hosannahs. "Wall Street now feels that business will continue along the same placid, prosperous lines it has held to for the past four years," explained the *Wall Street Journal*. "There has never been a President with a fundamental understanding of economics better than Mr. Hoover." In December 1928, Calvin Coolidge, peering down from the summit of eight years of prosperity, succumbed to irrational exuberance: "No Congress of the United States ever assembled on surveying the state of the Union, has met with a more pleasing prospect than that which appears at the present time."

In 1929, with the Dow at record highs, investment trusts began to be listed on the New York Stock Exchange at the rate of roughly one per day. With Wall Street aristocrats like J. P. Morgan embracing the formerly déclassé investment vehicles, investment trusts would raise $3 billion in 1929, bringing their total assets to $8 billion. Goldman, Sachs Trading Corp., which raised $100 million by selling shares at $100 apiece in December 1928, borrowed so that it could buy more stocks and shares in other similarly leveraged trusts. By February 7, it traded at $222.50, more than twice the value of the assets in its portfolio. Irving Fisher, the Yale economist and New Era avatar, formed an investment trust with two other elite economists, Joseph Davis of Stanford and Edmund Day of the University of Michigan. Like the gang of pointy-headed number crunchers behind Long-Term Capital Management, they believed a group of economists would inevitably trounce the market.

It's difficult to come up with data on the number of investors who were active in the market. But it was likely a small portion of the 123 million Americans held stock, 10 percent of households at most. The utility empire of Samuel Insull counted 600,000 shareholders and 50,000 bondholders. The member firms of twenty-nine exchanges in 1929 reported 1.55 million accounts, 600,000 of which traded on margin. A 1952 Brookings Institution study found that in 1930, forty-five common stocks collectively had 2.64 million shareholders of record. The number of shareholders was almost irrelevant, though. As in the 1990s, everybody was talking about the market. Groucho Marx was a huge investor, and so was Winston Churchill.

As in the 1990s, there were skeptics. Harvard economist William Z. Ripley warned in his 1927 book, *Main Street and Wall Street*, about pools of speculators who would rip the face off innocent investors. In early 1929, Charles Merrill, the founder of Merrill, Lynch, demanded that his firm sell off its holdings. "If I am wrong in insisting upon liquidation, then that is a luxury which I can afford and in which you and all of my partners should indulge me," he wrote. In 1929, Paul Warburg, one of the architects of the

Federal Reserve, warned that "when the savings of the masses are deposited as margins for stock exchange speculations, and when the extravagant use of funds for speculative purposes absorbs so much of the nation's credit supply that it threatens to cripple the country's regular business," the Fed should raise rates with alacrity. But such Chicken Littles were either ignored or attacked. Warburg, the fiscally moderate, phenomenally wealthy, Democratic-leaning Wall Street power—a precursor of Robert Rubin—was accused of being a tool of short-sellers.

Sadly, the Fed was an immature, new institution that lacked the fortitude and experience to know when to say no. In February, the New York Fed met and meekly decided to ask Washington for permission to raise rates from 5 percent to 6 percent. But Charles Mitchell of National City, who had become a governor of the New York Fed in January, had already discussed the necessity of leaving rates as they were with Treasury secretary Andrew Mellon. Permission was denied.

At this late date, the Fed was irrelevant. In late March, when stocks fell on concerns that the Fed would finally jack up rates to choke off speculation, the interest rate on call money spiked to 20 percent. Mitchell said National City would lend money at 15 percent, citing "an obligation which is paramount to any Federal Reserve warning, or anything else." The *New York Times* editorialized that "paying 15 per cent for money to speculate with ceases to be speculation and becomes insanity." In response to such warnings, William Crapo Durant, the founder of General Motors, who had become a major investor, in April purchased fifteen minutes of time on the Columbia Broadcasting System. His message was an early version of the plea that government should keep its grubby hands off Medicare: "Let the Federal Reserve Board keep its hands off business." Then, as now, the rich viewed cheap money for buying stocks as an entitlement.

The masses could get rich by buying stocks on margin, too. John J. Raskob, the former treasurer of General Motors, penned an article in the August 1929 *Ladies' Home Journal* titled "Everybody Ought to Be Rich." If Americans could plow $15 a week into stocks, he wrote, they'd have $80,000 at the end of ten years. Better yet, an investment company catering to individuals could take an investor's $200, borrow $300, buy $500 in stock, post the stock as collateral, and pay off the debt from dividends and from the sale of a few appreciated stocks. It would work, so long as existing trends continued. And why wouldn't they? Between March 1928 and September 1929 stocks doubled. On September 3, the Dow closed at 381.17. In the fall, economist Irving Fisher said, "Stock prices have reached what looks like a permanently high plateau." In its October 28 issue, *Time*, whose unerring capacity to front the conventional wisdom has long made it an excellent contrary indicator, put financier Ivar Krueger (known as the

Swedish Match King) on its cover. The following week, Samuel Insull graced the red-framed cover.

The crash happened the way marriages dissolve, slowly and then all at once. "When the crash finally came it came with a kind of surrealistic slowness," wrote *New Yorker* writer John Brooks in *Once in Golconda*, an elegant summary of the boom and bust. Throughout September and October, the market slipped downward. On Black Thursday, October 24, stocks fell as a record 12.89 million shares changed hands. Midday, Thomas Lamont of J. P. Morgan emerged from a meeting with bankers and noted that "there has been a little distress selling on the Stock Exchange." That's a close runner-up for understatement of the century. (The winner is Japanese emperor Hirohito's August 14, 1945, claim that "the war situation has developed not necessarily to Japan's advantage.")

The following Monday and Tuesday, the Dow lost nearly 30 percent in two trading days. But the carnage wasn't over, not by a long shot—in part thanks to all the leverage that had built up in the nation's financial system. Leverage, which had done so much to stimulate spending and investment, now exerted a powerful contractionary force. Banks, which took possession of securities from margined customers' accounts, started puking them up, stimulating further selling. Lenders of all sorts, realizing they'd have difficulty collecting on loans, stopped lending, which helped depress asset values across the board. "It would be hard to imagine a corporate system better designed to continue and accentuate a deflationary spiral," John Kenneth Galbraith wrote. Or as Ben Bernanke put it, "the credit squeeze helped convert the downturn of 1929–30 into a depression."

In the summer of 1930, Herbert Hoover told a group of clergy that "the depression is over." Other observers were less sanguine about the nation's prospects. "We are attacking capitalism all along the line and defeating it," Stalin proclaimed. *Da!* This wasn't just propaganda. Illiberal anticapitalist forces were everywhere on the march in 1930. In Germany's September 1930 election, the Nazis won 18 percent of the popular vote and saw their number of seats in the Reichstag soar from 12 to 107.

The evaporation of credit was a contagion that destroyed confidence the way the HIV virus destroys immune cells. "The whole complex of coin and currency, of credit and trust, was paralyzed because the trust was gone," wrote John Brooks. As banks failed, depositors lost money, nearly $800 million between 1930 and 1932. By 1933, nearly half of America's banks would fail. Starved of the fuel that had spurred growth during the 1920s, the economy contracted severely. Between 1929 and 1932, the average weekly wage fell from $25.03 to $16.73. National income fell from $87.4 billion in 1929 to $41.7 billion in 1932. The unemployment rate soared to 25 percent. In July 1932, when the nation's vast steel industry was running at an anemic 12 percent of capacity, the Dow had fallen more than 80 percent from its September 1929 high. Montgomery Ward was at 4, down from 138. Goldman, Sachs Trading Corp. sold for $1.75. Between 1929 and 1932, bond issuance fell 93 percent. The wheels of American capitalism ground to a halt.

Treasury secretary Andrew Mellon, displaying all the sensitivity of Barbara Bush in the Astrodome after Hurricane Katrina, thought the economic purging was all to the good. "High costs of living and high living will come down," he said. "People will work harder, live a more moral life." This, from a man who had just spent about $7 million to acquire about half of the best paintings in the collection of Russia's Hermitage museum, including a Raphael, a Velasquez, and a Titian. "Liquidate labor, liquidate stocks, liquidate the farmers, liquidate real estate" went Mellon's formulation. The American people's response was to liquidate Mellon and his fellow Republicans. In 1930, Democrats took control of the House for the first time since 1919. The 1932 election was like the Michael Jordan–led Dream Team taking on Angola in the 1992 Olympics. Roosevelt crushed Hoover in the popular vote 62.8 percent to 35 percent. The Democrats picked up ninety-seven House seats and twelve Senate seats, giving them enormous majorities.

Of course, control of the United States was no great prize in the spring of 1933. The system had ceased to function. By the spring of 1933, banks were open in only ten states. The bull market in stocks wasn't just dead. It was a festering, corrupt, maggot-ridden carcass. Many of the most admired CEOs, who had been splashed on magazine covers as financial innovators and seers in 1929, were felled by scandal. Ivar Kreuger shot himself in Paris on March 12, 1932. Samuel Insull, indicted for securities fraud, fled the country. Charles Mitchell was indicted in March 1933 for income tax avoidance. The partners of J. P. Morgan, it was revealed, paid no income taxes in 1931 and 1932. Congressional investigations revealed Wall Street to be a tangled nest of conflicts of interest. How bad was it? Just imagine how damaging it would be to the psyche of investors if in, say, 2002, after a big crash, the heads of cutting-edge firms like Enron, conglomerates like Tyco, and well-known analysts at Citigroup were all revealed to be a bunch of two-bit hacks and petty thieves.

In response to such revelations, Richard Whitney, the patrician head of the New York Stock Exchange (Groton, '07, Harvard, '11), blamed the government for the financial distress and suggested the administration balance the budgets by cutting pensions for veterans. Whitney, who had dubbed the exchange a "perfect institution," would later be busted for grand larceny and serve time in Sing Sing. Among his crimes: stealing from the NYSE's gratuity fund and, the ultimate in WASP betrayal, embezzling from the New York Yacht Club.

Onto this postapocalyptic scene of devastation strode Franklin Delano Roosevelt. FDR has come in for plenty of grief from modern historians, and especially from pseudo-historians. Those on the right will never forgive FDR his successes in reviving the American economy and saving capitalism through government intervention, while those on the left deem his actions too tame and will never forgive him his failures on issues like segregation. But there's a reason that many historians still regard FDR, for all his faults (he was merely a great man, not a saint), as the greatest twentieth-century president. FDR's four terms comprise a remarkable sustained period of national greatness, lasting accomplishments ranging from electrifying the country to Social Security, defeating Fascism, and liberating Europe. The complaints from present-day writers that he burdened the economy with regulations and high taxes are deeply ahistorical. In the 1930s, after all, the third way between liberal democratic capitalism, which had so miserably failed in the West and the expanding Soviet system of tyrannical communism was the brand of national socialism ascendant in Germany, Italy, and Japan. And we all know how well that turned out.

The New Dealers sought to revive and repair the shattered mechanisms of private capital by erecting a set of regulations, insurance schemes, and government backstops—some temporary, some permanent—intended to boost confidence. But while the New Deal's economic policies would occasionally involve clumsy overreaching, the initial response to the financial crisis was hardly radical.

"The proposal adds to the ancient rule of caveat emptor, the further doctrine: 'let the seller beware,' " Roosevelt said of the Securities Act of 1933, which was approved in the summer of 1933. "It puts the burden of telling the whole truth on the seller." The government didn't want to stop people from speculating, "in as much as many of the industrial developments in the country began as speculations," said Huston Thompson, who helped draft the Securities Act (and who clearly recognized the importance of the Pop! dynamic). The act required companies selling stocks or bonds to the public to file statements with the Federal Trade Commission, and to file prospectuses containing data about company operations, legal issues, and their officers. Directors and executives who signed off on such statements could be held liable if they contained false information. The act exempted securities already issued, as well as those issued by government and railroads. Harvard law professor and future Supreme Court Justice Felix Frankfurter, writing in *Fortune*, correctly called it "a belated and conservative attempt to curb the recurrence of old abuses."

The Securities Exchange Act of 1934 created a new body—the Securities and Exchange Commission—to enforce these rules and make new ones, and to regulate the stock exchanges. It also directed the Federal Reserve to implement new standards on margin lending and required companies to file audited reports—a development that would be crucial for the emerging science of stock analysis.

(That year, Benjamin Graham, a Columbia finance professor, and his teaching assistant, David Dodd, first turned Graham's notes into a book that has become the bible of value investors like Warren Buffett: *Security Analysis*.) And rather than installing a left-wing industry scourge at the SEC's helm, Roosevelt would ultimately appoint Joseph Kennedy, an experienced stock operator.

These mild actions were much too much for Wall Street bankers, who were singularly unchastened by their spectacular failure. A public relations team led by Edward Bernays (the nephew of Sigmund Freud) and former Rockefeller consigliere Ivy Lee led a vicious campaign against any and all regulations, in which they accused FDR and his crowd of being nothing more than a bunch of freedom-hating communists. To prove that the regulations would hamper capital formation, investment banks stopped issuing stocks and bonds. In January 1935, only $11 million in new securities were registered with the SEC, down from $113 million in July 1934, when it began operations. Of course, people who work on 6 percent commission refusing to sell were like disease-ridden prostitutes taking a vow of celibacy. They suffered economically even as they contributed to the improvement of public health. (After all, about half of the $50 billion in new securities Wall Street had sold in the ten years after World War I had turned out to be worthless.) The capital strike ended on March 7, 1935, when Swift & Co., the meat-packing company founded in the 1880s, registered a $43 million bond issue. Wall Street was back in business.

The banking system would require more direct assistance. On March 7, 1933, Roosevelt declared a national bank holiday, which was a little like calling the opening day of deer season a game holiday. Many of those that closed never reopened. Under the Emergency Banking Act, passed on March 9, 1933, the government began to provide capital to banks. The main goal of these early efforts was to force banks to insulate their customers—depositors—from the reckless credit practices of the 1920s boom. The Banking Act of 1933, passed in June, forced banks to get out of the stock-lending business by divorcing commercial banking from the securities business. The act also created the Federal Deposit Insurance Corporation. The lack of adequate risk management and credit insurance had contributed mightily to the credit death spiral. And so, if banks were going to be a part of the Federal Reserve system, the government said, they'd have to buy some insurance on their deposits. The bargain: banks were assessed a premium of 0.5 percent of deposits, and in exchange the FDIC would insure deposits up to a cap of $2,500 (raised to $5,000 in 1934). Naturally, the bankers, most of whom had failed to carry out their fiduciary responsibilities to stockholders and customers, dubbed the FDIC a horrific intrusion. Francis Sisson, president of the American Bankers Association, urged his fellow bankers to oppose deposit insurance, which he dubbed "unsound, unscientific, unjust, and dangerous." After all, "overwhelming opinions of experienced bankers are emphatically opposed to deposit guaranties which compel strong and well managed banks to pay the losses of the weak."

The measure passed, and insurance went into effect in January 1934. Lo and behold, it worked. Total commercial bank deposits rose by a whopping $7.2 billion in 1934, or 22 percent. "With this one piece of legislation the fear which operated so efficiently to transmit weakness was dissolved," wrote John Kenneth Galbraith. "Rarely has so much been accomplished by a single law." The law didn't stop banks from failing. But because depositors were made whole when banks did fail, the FDIC stopped isolated failures from spawning paralyzing industry-wide runs, at minimal cost to the banks. A final crucial measure came in 1935, when yet another banking act reorganized the Federal Reserve and centralized policy-making in Washington. It would no longer be possible for the Federal Reserve Bank of New York, unduly influenced by Wall Street bankers gorging on cheap money, to maintain its own monetary policy.

Home lending was the third credit-related sector in need of salvage. In 1933, the mortgage business was almost as bad off as Wall Street and the banking industry. "By early 1933, more than 40 percent of the country's $20 billion in home mortgages were in default," wrote historian John

Olson. And lenders weren't exactly flooding the mailboxes of struggling homeowners with re-fi offers. Life insurance companies, which had extended $525 million in mortgage loans in 1929, made a mere $10 million in new loans in 1933. In June 1933, Congress created the Home Owner's Loan Corporation, which allowed individuals to refinance up to $14,000 of mortgage debt with a fifteen-year, 5 percent government mortgage. In short order, the HOLC lent about $3.1 billion to more than 1 million people, effectively refinancing one in every five nonfarm-owner-occupied dwellings. Next, the National Housing Act of 1934 created the Federal Savings and Loan Insurance Corporation, which insured deposits in savings and loans institutions. "To the extent that the home mortgage market did function in the years immediately following 1933, it was largely due to the direct involvement of the federal government," Ben Bernanke concluded.

In the 1920s, once an institution made a loan, it stayed on the books, tying up capital and inhibiting lending during down cycles. There was no effective secondary market for home mortgages. So in 1938, the government chartered the Federal National Mortgage Association. Fannie Mae, which could borrow money cheaply, and raise funds to buy and sell mortgages that were insured by the Federal Housing Administration, thus taking loans off lenders' books and replenishing capital.

The alphabet soup of New Deal initiatives contained

other items that helped forge a new financial infrastructure. In 1938, the SEC forced a reorganization of the New York Stock Exchange, under which the Exchange added three representatives of public investors to its board and named a full-time president to run the operation. One of the final acts of the New Deal came in 1940, with the Investment Company Act, which provided the first layer of regulation on investment companies. Once again, the mandates were relatively mild given the sins committed by investment trusts in the 1920s: disclosure standards, a requirement that 40 percent of each firm's directors be outsiders, and the imposition of liability for directors and officers.

As with the railroad and the telegraph, this new commercial infrastructure set the stage for entrepreneurs with new business models to go to work. And eventually, the cycle of consolidation, innovation, and growth began to kick in. Among the first was a consolidator, Charles Merrill. Having tried to build a firm catering to individuals in the 1920s, Merrill got out of the brokerage business in the early 1930s and spent the Depression watching over his investments in Safeway, the big grocery chain. But in early 1940, when Wall Street volume was shriveling, Merrill made one of the great contrarian moves of all time. He spent $2.5 million to acquire control of E. A. Pierce & Co., one of the largest surviving brokerage firms, with branches in ninety-three cities. Like Roosevelt, Merrill saw disclosure as the key to reestablishing shattered confidence. In 1941, his new firm, redubbed Merrill, Lynch, published an annual report. And by publishing a newspaper and information-laden ads, he aimed to educate investors about securities. By 1944, Merrill, Lynch accounted for 10 percent of the New York Stock Exchange's daily volume and had 250,000 customer accounts.

As Americans gingerly began to dip their scalded toes back into the investment pool, a new class of companies arose to service the new users. With new funds forming, the mutual fund industry grew from $450 million in assets and 296,000 accounts in 1940 to $2.53 billion in assets and 938,000 accounts in 1950. In 1946, Boston-based investor Edward C. Johnson II founded Fidelity Investments. Two years later, Alfred Jones, a former reporter at *Fortune*, formed the first long-short hedge fund. It took a long time for a critical mass of shareholders to grow, in part because the scars were so deep. The Dow did not surpass its September 1929 high until November 23, 1954. And in 1952, the Brookings Institution found that only 6.49 million people held publicly owned stocks out of a population of 155.5 million—4.2 percent.

World War II put a crimp in consumer spending. But when the soldiers returned home, consumer credit began to revive, fueled by banks and a series of new products. The first credit card, Diners Club, was introduced in 1950. Pent-up war-time savings were unleashed. As young families moved into and began to furnish houses in the suburbs, consumer credit rose from $2.5 billion in 1950 to $45 billion in 1960. In 1958, Bank of America kicked off a new era of spending and lending as it bombed Fresno, California, with 50,000 offers for a new credit card.

Far from hampering the growth of the securities, credit, and housing complexes, the New Deal–era regime of light regulation, disclosure, and enforcement—much of which remains intact—helped spur the massive growth of these industries in the decades since World War II. In fact, the matrix of backstops and insurance, regulation, and behavior modification through disclosure helps give the U.S. economy its distinctive flavor. And it's hard not to conclude that the post-credit-bubble efforts of the 1930s laid the groundwork for the remarkable growth of the consumer-driven economy and for the nation's financial dominance in the second half of the twentieth century. Look at the numbers. Since the summer of 1933, the Dow Jones Industrial Average has risen by a factor of 284. The value of stocks traded on U.S. exchanges has risen from $58.3 billion in 1938 to about $16 trillion today. The banking industry, essentially dead in 1933, is alive and well. "No depositor has lost a single cent of FDIC-insured funds as a result of a failure," notes the FDIC, which now insures $4.1 trillion in deposits. Some things haven't changed, of course. The same types of self-defeating investment bankers who railed against the post-bust Securities Acts of 1933 and 1934 railed against the post-bust

Sarbanes-Oxley Act of 2002, using much the same language.

More broadly, the U.S. economy is today characterized by a broad socialization of risk through credit insurance and through the securitization of all types of assets—jumbo and subprime mortgages, car loans, credit card receivables, and student loans. The SEC, the strengthened Fed, Fannie Mae, the FDIC—all these components of the new financial infrastructure continue to provide Americans with the confidence to borrow, to lend, to invest, and to take risks. Again, the differences between the United States and Europe are instructive. In 1930, Germany and the United States had the same rate of stock ownership. Today, about half of Americans own stock while only 10 percent of Germans do. New York remains the world's financial capital, despite challenges from London, Hong Kong, and Tokyo. Americans enjoy unparalleled access to credit, and U.S. capital markets are the largest and most transparent in the world. The constituents of the so-called FIRE complex—finance, insurance, and real estate—today account for 20 percent of the economy and 20 percent of the capitalization of the S&P 500. All are built on the infrastructure of a sound banking system, transparent and lightly regulated capital markets, and a robust home lending system. And all continue to benefit from direct and indirect government backing.

To be sure, FDR and the New Dealers didn't lick the

business cycle. During the recession of 1937–1938, one in five Americans was out of work. The New Dealers also couldn't lick the American capacity for willful delusion when it comes to investing. Like a cicada, the Pop! impulse would lie dormant for more than half a century before surfacing with a vengeance in the next New Era. The wounds from the 1929 crash and the Depression were certainly deep, and they conditioned behavior for the decades that followed. But time heals all wounds, and the bubble-blowing tendency was bound to resurface. "During any future boom some newly rediscovered virtuosity of the free enterprise system will be cited," John Kenneth Galbraith predicted in 1955. "It will be pointed out that people are justified in paying the present prices—indeed, almost any price—to have an equity position in the system." Some will speak against the speculation and call for the Federal Reserve and other powers to act, but others, like Charles Mitchell, will urge that the good times roll: "The newspapers, some of them, will agree and speak harshly of those who think action might be in order," Galbraith concluded. "They will be called men of little faith."

5

THE INTERNET

Karl Marx wrote that history reveals itself first as tragedy, and then a second time as farce. If that's the case, the 1990s were an Adam Sandler movie. And not one of the bearable ones, like *The Wedding Singer*. No, one of the truly awful ones, like *Happy Gilmore*. Looking back on the bubble and bust surrounding information technology, e-commerce, and everything Internet-related is painful to rehash, and even more painful to relive. To a man and woman, those who survived the roller-coaster ride of the 1990s will earnestly testify that none had ever seen the likes of what took place in those last feverish years of the second millennium: the greed and conflicts of interest on Wall Street, the misguided investments, the rampant hubris, the dopey extrapolation of short-term trends into the distant future, the irrational exuberance.

Except they had. For in the 1990s, the themes from the prior Pop! episodes came together. Spurred by the putative need for infinite bandwidth, the promise of interactive television and computing, and the exponential growth of the Internet and e-commerce, companies rushed (yet again!) to build a new commercial and consumer infrastructure. Like the telegraph, the Internet was a network communications technology that transmitted data at the speed of light. Like the railroad, it was a pervasive infrastructure, much of it built across commercially empty space, that could be used to deliver newfangled goods and services. And as in the 1920s, investors, egged on by promoters and philosophers who proclaimed a new economic era, collectively lost their heads—and then collectively lost their Banana Republic shirts.

As in bubbles past, government played something of a role. Al Gore may not have invented the Internet, but some other government employees did. The original network of computers that would form the Internet, ARPANET, the Advanced Research Projects Agency Network, was funded by the Defense Department in the 1960s and 1970s. Mosaic, the first Web browser, was invented in 1992 at the National Center for Supercomputing Applications, a University of Illinois facility funded by the National Science Foundation. And the rollout of the Internet in the 1990s was carried out in large part by companies operating in regulated industries such as telecommunications and cable.

The National Bureau of Economic Research, which retroactively decrees when recessions start and when they end, does not date booms, manias, bubbles, and busts. But the consensus holds that the Internet boom kicked off with the initial public offering of Netscape, the Web browser company, on August 9, 1995. The bubble rapidly gathered critical mass because Netscape and its followers were able to plug into a pair of large installed bases. By 1995, the United States boasted 150 million personal computers, a growing number of which were connected to the World Wide Web (as the Internet was known in the mid-1990s). In 1994, America Online (as AOL used to be known in the mid-1990s) already had 1.4 million members.

By the mid-1990s, the United States also sported the world's largest installed base of investors. The investor class finally began to grow during the 1980s bull market; by 1990, 23 percent of households owned stocks or mutual funds. But in the 1990s, thanks to the continuing 401(k) revolution, the rise of discount brokers, and a raging bull market, the legions grew into hordes. By 2000, 48 percent of U.S. households would own mutual funds. No other nation on earth had a more intense and broad culture of investing. So while prior U.S. investment bubbles had relied on ad hoc capital—local subscriptions for the telegraph, government aid and foreign bondholders for the railroads, a small number of domestic stockholders trading on margin in the 1920s—the 1990s booms were fueled, directly and indirectly, by individual investors. Domestic stock and bondholders interacted powerfully with venture capitalists and investment banks, who had, contrary to the keening doomsayers of the 1930s, thrived on the infrastructure erected during the New Deal.

As in the 1920s, the Federal Reserve facilitated the provision of cheap capital. As was not the case in the 1920s, the Fed was a strong, confident institution led by a man whose stature grew in a logarithmic relationship to the stock market. When Federal Reserve chairman Alan Greenspan spoke (or didn't speak), the markets listened. During the boom, Greenspan would provide crucial intellectual support to investors. Congress chipped in as well. The Telecommunications Act of 1996 changed the rules of the game to encourage a huge amount of speculative investing. The act allowed local phone companies to enter the long-distance market, and long-distance firms like AT&T and MCI to enter the local phone markets. What's more, it forced owners of local networks to make their wires available to Internet service providers at relatively low costs. As a result, "the platform became a common in which creativity flourished," as former Federal Communications Commission chairman Reed Hundt put it. "This led to the lowest-priced Internet access in the world. Given America's large installed base of computers, the result was that the Internet became an American phenomenon." American exceptionalism, once again.

Om Malik's *Broadbandits* (2003) comprehensively documents the rise in the latter half of the 1990s of a huge bubble surrounding the nuts and bolts of the Internet—fiber-optic systems, equipment, and the services to run them. It was Methodless Enthusiasm 3.0. Network businesses came out of nowhere, raised huge sums of capital, and sank the capital into the ground. They did so in part because techno-pundits spun wonderful tales about convergence, the delivery of movies by Internet, and interactive television—all of which would create massive demand. UUNET, the Internet backbone provider acquired by WorldCom in 1996, developed data suggesting that Internet traffic doubled every hundred days. A more sober paper, by Andrew Odlyzsko and Kerry Coffman at AT&T Labs, published in October 1998, concluded that in fact traffic was rising between 70 and 150 percent each year.

The marketplace believed New Economy UUNET, not Old Economy AT&T. After all, UUNET's parent, WorldCom, led the nation in bandwidth in 1998. Its CEO, Canada-born, Mississippi-based, Bible-thumping, long-haired Bernie Ebbers, was only one of many burgeoning bandwidth magnates. Gary Winnick, the founder of Global Crossing, who cultivated a somewhat less down-home style, made Henry O'Reilly look like a sober, risk-averse engineer. Winnick, a former Drexel Burnham Lambert junk bond salesman, set about to construct a 100,000-mile global fiber-optic network, which he would sell or lease in pieces to telephone companies. Founded in March 1997, Global Crossing raised $399 million in its August 1998 initial public offering, and returned to the capital markets like a famished diner at the Golden Corral all-you-can-eat buffet. Winnick gorged himself, too, selling $735 million of the company's stock. In 2000, he spent $65 million to purchase a 23,000-square-foot pile in Bel Air, Casa Encantada (which is Spanish for "this house is only half as large as Aaron Spelling's") and spent millions renovating it.

There were more copycats than can be found in Beijing's Silk Alley: Qwest and 360networks, Enron and Williams Communications, and PSINet. "Mind-boggling miles of fiber-optic cable are being laid in the U.S. every day," *Plunkett's Telecommunications Industry Almanac* reported in 2000. Between 1996 and 2001, according to KMI Research, 80.2 million miles of optical fiber were installed in the United States—more than three-quarters of the total ever built. And the United States accounted for an astonishing 40 percent of the world's optical-fiber and cable market. The cost: a lot. As Roger Lowenstein wrote in *Origins of the Crash*: "In the half-decade after deregulation, telecom companies borrowed $1.6 trillion from banks and enlisted Wall Street to sell $600 billion in bonds."

Contractors buried cable alongside old railroad rights-of-way and assiduously dug up city streets to install new fiber-optic lines. But as was the case with the telegraph, the uptake was sometimes a little slow. The company @Home, hatched in 1995 to sell high-speed Internet service through cable companies, promised to have 1 million subscribers by the end of 1996. By March 1998, it had only 90,000. Connectivity remained a problem. Data would travel remarkably fast across oceans or across the country, but would encounter roadblocks in the last mile as cable and telephone companies labored to rewire homes. And while the prices for the commodities needed to build networks rose, the excess capacity that rapidly developed ensured that companies would have little pricing power. The title of biggest bandwidth provider in the country was thus more a liability than an asset. "What Ebbers didn't know was that he was the biggest fool in telecomville," Om Malik wrote. "No one was making meaningful money from bandwidth and data networks, because they were too expensive to build, manage, and upgrade." UUNET would lease a T1 connection from a local phone company for $2,000 per month and then resell it to customers for $1,500 per month. In *Apocalypse Now*, Martin Sheen's Captain Willard engages in a riveting dialogue with Marlon Brando's Colonel Kurtz:

> **Willard:** They told me that you had gone totally insane, and that your methods were unsound.
> **Kurtz:** Are my methods unsound?
> **Willard:** I don't see any method at all, sir.

Just so, it was nearly impossible to detect any method in WorldCom's business model.

The fiber-optic networks fell prey to the same cycle that had felled the railroads a century before. Vicious competition and high fixed costs meant companies ran at negative margins. As in the 1880s, the network companies responded by (a) expanding and (b) cheating. Global Crossing, which was having difficulty making profits, started Asia Global Crossing. Global Crossing and many other companies engaged in shady capacity swaps, which allowed firms to book exchanges of capacity as revenues. MCI

WorldCom simply concocted earnings on a breathtaking scale, manufacturing some $9 billion in profits between 1999 and 2002. In so doing, the market leader forced the few in the industry using honest accounting methods to cut prices and lose money. In hindsight, all these companies were doomed in 1998 and 1999. But investors had no clue. In the spring of 2000, Global Crossing had a $45 billion market capitalization. WorldCom's market value peaked at more than $175 billion in 1999.

The fiber-optic bubble was only half the story. For at the same time, excessive, irrational, and methodless investment flowed into companies that aimed to use the Internet to deliver new types of services. The dot-coms made some investment in hard assets: loftlike office space, computers and servers, Aeron chairs, cool messenger-style laptop bags, kegs. And they spent wildly to build up their own infrastructure: Web sites, warehouses, and fulfillment systems. But the New Economy called for people to shop, read, and entertain themselves in fundamentally new ways. Convincing consumers that it was safe, sensible, and efficient to buy groceries, airplane tickets and cruises, mutual funds, prescription drugs and pet food, fine chocolates and jewelry, used cars and clothes via the Internet necessitated the creation of a new mindset. And so a great deal of money was spent building a new cultural and psychological infrastructure.

Many start-ups thus forked out a huge chunk of their

venture capital and IPO money building mind share and buying advertising on television, and in magazines and newspapers. The result: New Economy magazines like *Wired*, the *Industry Standard*, and *Red Herring* and Old Economy warhorses like *Fortune*, *BusinessWeek*, and *Forbes* grew fat like the September *Vogue*.

Given the growing frenzy surrounding the Internet, excess capacity developed quickly. In any market segment, if one dot-com appeared, three or four were sure to follow: E*Trade, Ameritrade, and TD Waterhouse in the brokerage world; Orbitz, Hotwire, and Expedia in the travel sphere. And the competition didn't arise only from other venture-backed companies. Amazon, which, like Montgomery Ward and Sears in the 1880s, set out to build a high-volume mail-order catalog, entered a field in which Montgomery Ward and Sears already had staked out positions. As the 1990s wore on, and as bricks-and-mortar incumbents began to fight back with their own Web operations, Amazon.com and Petsdirect.com and Drugstore.com faced some tough competition.

This competition spurred further investments in mental infrastructure—price wars, incentives, inducements of all types. Amazon essentially ran its business at negative margins to gain critical mass and customer loyalty. It offered discounted prices *and* free shipping and delivery, sort of like what railroads did in the 1880s. Other companies ran ridiculous promotions. For a period, one online brokerage offered customers $400 cash if they would open an account with a minimum balance of $1,000. By 1999, the Web had become a cheapskate's paradise. E-mails and coupons offering freebies, discounts, and cash rebates circulated like bongs at a fraternity party. Online publications, eager to build audiences, gave away content for free or found it difficult to charge meaningful subscription rates. All the activity sucked in investors and users. Amazon had served 17 million customers by 1999. That it lost money on pretty much every transaction was beside the point.

Unsound methods? Sure. But it didn't matter. Things were different this time. Irving Fisher was dead and buried, but the concept of a New Era was alive and well, or so said the era's most prominent economist. "It is safe to say that we are witnessing this decade in the United States, history's most compelling demonstration of free peoples operating in free markets," Alan Greenspan exulted on September 8, 1999, when the Dow stood at 11,036 and the NASDAQ stood at 2,808. With inflation licked, and the business cycles an unfortunate phenomenon last seen in the early 1990s, like Vanilla Ice, risk was banished. Stocks were an asset class that returned absolutely nothing in nominal terms between 1929 and 1954, and again between 1966 and 1981. But that was then. This was now. And now stocks were fail-safe investments. Among the tomes available for sale on Amazon.com were not just one that promised the Dow would go to 36,000 in "perhaps three to five years" (*Dow 36,000*, 1999), but one that promised the Dow would go to 40,000 (*Dow 40,000*, 1998) and one that promised that the Dow would go to 100,000 (*Dow 100,000: Fact or Fiction*, 1999). These were simply a modest extension of recent trends: between 1995 and 1999, the NASDAQ averaged a 40 percent annual return. Stocks like Amazon just needed a few years to grow into their pro forma projections.

The daily parade of bull-market celebrities appearing on CNBC hammered home the point that it was always a good time to buy stocks, at pretty much any price. Abby Joseph Cohen of Goldman, Sachs, and Joseph Battipaglia of Gruntal & Co., latter-day sages of Fort Lee, New Jersey, the home of CNBC, proclaimed every dip a buying opportunity. Instead of investment trusts, we had go-go mutual funds like the Kinetics Internet Fund, run by baby-faced Ryan Jacob, which notched a 198 percent return in 1998, and publicly held Internet incubators like CMGI, which launched start-ups the way clowns blow soap bubbles at kids' birthday parties.

The blessings of the Internet extended far beyond stocks. In his 1997 book *What Will Be*, MIT computer scientist Michael Dertouzos prophesied that the Net "may help stave off future flare-ups of ethnic hatred and national break-ups." (He wasn't any more accurate about that than David Sarnoff had been when he suggested radio would perform the same function.) In his 2000 book, *Telecosm:*

How Infinite Bandwidth Will Revolutionize Our World, George Gilder wrote that the theories of pessimistic British economist Thomas Malthus were toast. "For most of human history, most people have believed that economics is essentially a zero-sum game—that scarcity will ultimately prevail over abundance," he wrote. No longer. In an age where bandwidth was infinite and free, everything would be hunky-dory—and the stocks he plugged, among them WorldCom and Global Crossing, would go straight to the moon.

The United States of America, of course, was the center of this shiny, happy, prosperous universe, a bulwark of stability, growth, low inflation, and productivity, an economic powerhouse blessed with economic superheroes. Among them were Federal Reserve chairman Alan Greenspan, lionized by Bob Woodward in the best-selling 2000 hagiography *Maestro*. With Greenspan and his fellow technocrats at the helm—*Time* in February 1999 dubbed Greenspan, Treasury Secretary Robert Rubin, and Deputy Treasury Secretary Larry Summers the Committee to Save the World—the United States would suffer no bear markets. And thanks to the Internet, there would be no more recessions. After all, the speed of communications gave managers near-perfect knowledge of their markets and the ability to manage supply chains in real time. Which is pretty much exactly what William Orton of Western Union said back in 1870.

As in the 1920s, there were skeptics. But they were cranks, sore losers, dorks who insisted on wearing ties when everybody—even the cuff-linked private equity mandarins—was going casual. They were booked on CNBC for the same reason P. T. Barnum hired bearded ladies, as freakish historical curiosities. Alan Abelson, *Barron's'* acerbic lead columnist, argued in the January 25, 1999, issue that "the pipeline of new offerings, chock-a-block with Web thises and dot-com thats (WebTrends, ZDNet, pcOrder.com, Priceline.com, and MiningCo.com, to name only a few), could well bury the group." James Grant of *Grant's Interest Rate Observer* spent much of the late 1990s hacking away at the pillars of the New Economy faith. (He even argued, heretically, in a September 1998 *Wall Street Journal* article that "Alan Greenspan Isn't God.") Despite the *fatwas* issued by enraged bond mullahs, Grant managed to survive the decade.

Executives who refused to cannibalize their own businesses were similarly relegated to the Old Economy scrap heap, treated daily to unflattering comparisons to two-year-old, profitless companies run by Stanford MBAs. Tiffany & Co. spent a century building up a perfectly good brand and a massive global business. With $1.4 billion in annual sales, it was worth about $2.2 billion in the fall of 1999. In September 1999, online jeweler Ashford.com went public and was quickly rewarded with a $1.5 billion market cap, even though its business was not solid as a rock. In the year ending March 2000, it lost $72 million on sales of $40 million. A favorite parlor game was to take the stock market value of a dot-com highflyer like Yahoo! and calculate how many times over it could buy Ford or General Motors.

By 1999, the melt-up was in full swing. To a large degree, the dot-com/bull market mentality pervaded popular culture. Darren Star, creator of *Beverly Hills, 90210*; *Melrose Place*; and *Sex and the City*, in the summer of 2000 cooked up a new series, *The $treet*. James Cramer, the hedge fund manager and founder of TheStreet.com, appeared in ads for Rockport shoes. Tina Brown described her buzzy new magazine, *Talk*, as a "cultural search engine." Entrepreneurs began to raise money in ever-larger gulps. Webvan, the online grocer backed by Louis Borders, the cofounder of Borders Books, plowed $1.3 billion into the creation of a huge network of warehouses. The praise lavished on entrepreneurs became more fulsome and ripe. *Forbes* in May 1999 wondered whether Priceline.com founder Jay Walker was "An Edison for a New Age?" Michael Saylor, the thirty-something founder of business intelligence software company MicroStrategy (1999 revenues: $151 million) in March 2000 pledged to spend $100 million to build an online university. Many of the businesses launched in 1999 and 2000 were Farrelly brothers concepts: dumb and dumber. Bill Gross, the impresario behind incubator Idealab, launched Free-PC.com, which gave PCs to people who would consent to look at online ads.

AllAdvantage.com, formed in 1999, raised $200 million. The business plan rested in part on paying people fifty cents an hour to surf the Internet and look at ads.

The years 1999 and 2000 saw 69 percent of the venture technology funding of the 1975–2000 period, as well as 55 percent of the public technology funding. Technology, to a large degree, became the market, accounting for 37 percent of the S&P 500, up from 8 percent in 1989. And the hot tech stocks were finding their way into a growing number of portfolios. The S&P 500, which brings in new companies only after they attain a market capitalization of $4 billion or more, acted like a weir for dot-com minnows that had suddenly become whales. AOL entered at the end of 1998 at 155, Global Crossing was welcomed to the club on September 28, 1999, at 26, and Yahoo! on December 7, 1999, at 228. Of the 58 stocks entering the index in 2000, twenty-four were NASDAQ stocks.

Of course, it was all too much, too soon. There wasn't enough traffic to fill all those pipes. It turned out that enough fiber-optic cable was laid in the 1990s for one or two generations of Internet users. On most days in 2001, just 5 percent of the nation's fiber-optic capacity was being used. And there wasn't enough e-commerce to go around. Pro forma disease had become epidemic. Every business plan and prospectus called for CompanyX.com to gain 10 percent of market share within five years, in a market that was growing at a 50 percent compound rate. But it turned out that there were nineteen other companies in the same space, each of which planned on doing what was necessary to gain a 10 percent market share. And it turned out that the market was growing at only a 25 percent compound rate. There was no way to make the numbers add up.

Another problem: for all the spending, the infrastructure wasn't quite there. A telegraph-based stock ticker would have failed in the 1840s, when data still had to be shipped across the Hudson by ferry. So, too, would a mail-order business in the 1860s, when railroads ran on different gauges. Many of the 1990s-vintage start-ups had high-speed business models. But too many of their potential customers were running on 56K modems. In December 1999, according to the Federal Communications Commission, there were only 2.75 million high-speed lines in the United States, 1.8 million of them residential. The Pew Internet & American Life Project found that in June 2000, fewer than 5 percent of Americans had broadband at home. The slow pace at which Time Warner Cable rolled out Road Runner, its high-speed service, inspired a new form of neighborhood envy in New York. It was the first time in history that Upper East Side denizens looked out their windows, wistfully wishing they lived in the South Bronx (which got wired for high-speed Internet first). All of which made many ideas unworkable. I still recall the hour I spent testing Priceline's early grocery-shopping service on my home dial-up connection in 1999. It took forever to scroll through the items, name my price, and print out the list. I walked to the grocery store, only to find it didn't have half the items. A frictionless business! It was like break-dancing on a shag carpet while wearing a corduroy suit.

In retrospect, the signs of the top were easy to spot. The *Time* magazine cover on December 27, 1999, declaring Amazon founder Jeffrey Bezos Man of the Year. The announcement of the AOL–Time Warner merger on January 10, 2000. The 349-point fall in the NASDAQ on April 3, 2000. As some Christians hoped and techno–Chicken Littles feared, the apocalypse did come in 2000. It just didn't come in January. Between March 10 and May 17, the NASDAQ fell 37 percent. The process that had helped inflate Internet stocks and Internet companies started to reverse, and all the myths of the 1990s were rudely shattered. The business cycle returned, as the economy briefly slipped into recession in 2001. The value destruction was massive. Between December 31, 1999, and July 12, 2001, 362 pure-play Internet companies saw their market cap plummet from $1.142 trillion to $415 billion. The NASDAQ fell a sickening 78 percent from March 2000 to October 2002.

It was like Little Big Horn. Fiber-optic and dot-com companies failed left and right: eToys and Exodus Communications, Webvan and PSINet, Global Crossing and Kozmo .com, 360networks and MCI WorldCom. Many of the formerly swaggering survivors—Amazon and Yahoo!, Gateway and AOL—were on life support. Om Malik concluded that in the telecom sector alone, more than a hundred companies went bankrupt, wiping out $750 billion in market value and 600,000 jobs. All that was left of many dreams were vacant offices and a healthy secondary market in Aeron chairs.

Just as in prior postbubble periods, scandals engulfed some of the most prominent executives in the industry. Wall Street was revealed to be a thicket of conflicts of interest. Ace telecom analyst Jack Grubman of Citigroup was endorsing stocks to gain investment banking business (and preschool admission for his children). Über-tech banker Frank Quattrone of Credit Suisse First Boston buttered up tech executives by funneling hot IPOs to them. Executives who had graced the front pages of *Forbes*, *Fortune*, and *BusinessWeek*, like Kenneth Lay of Enron and Bernie Ebbers of WorldCom, were revealed to be common crooks. Once again, the Dick at the helm of the New York Stock Exchange came under investigation: this time it was Grasso, not Whitney. And just as in the 1920s, the airing of widespread conflicts of interest on Wall Street led to embarrassing hearings and calls for reform. Instead of the Securities Act of 1933, we got the Sarbanes-Oxley Act and the call to treat options as expenses.

The culture turned swiftly against the dot-com era. Philip Caplan's dot-com dead pool site, F*****company .com, became one of the first blogs. Robert Shiller's *Irrational Exuberance* quickly replaced *Dow 36,000* on the best-seller list. The ratings of CNBC plunged, and bulls like Abby Joseph Cohen assumed the media profile of Karl Rove after the November 2006 election. *Red Herring* and the *Industry Standard* disappeared. Schadenfreude levels remained in a permanently elevated state, to be surpassed only in Boston when the Red Sox beat the Yankees in seven games in the 2004 American League Championship Series. By mid-2002, conventional wisdom held that the whole thing had been an unambiguous disaster, a scam, a waste of time and money.

Or had it? This boom and bust took place on Internet time—faster, bigger, louder, more arrogant and cocksure than previous cycles. But so too did the postbust cycle of innovation, recovery, and growth. The tanking NASDAQ may have brought the string of IPOs to a halt, and the bankruptcies caused venture capitalists to curb their enthusiasm. But people didn't stop sending e-mails, installing broadband connections, or shopping online. Despite their failures as stocks, these companies had succeeded in creating a national broadband infrastructure almost overnight. The manic marketing efforts had coaxed millions of people to open accounts and become comfortable with making transactions online.

In the postbust period, the prices of everything associated with the technology and the Internet continued to plunge. And excess capacity was only part of the story. Moore's law dictated that computer processing power got cheaper each year, and the price of storage fell each year. So, too, did the prices of the building blocks of online businesses: servers and digital cameras, Internet name registration and Web design, Web-hosting and e-mail. *Forbes* publisher Rich Karlgaard in April 2003 coined the phrase "The Cheap Revolution" to define these powerful developments, which were bad news for hardware companies like Sun Microsystems and EMC but great news for consumers. Prices of these service and goods didn't rise once the economy recovered, in part because of excess capacity. The median price for a standard unit of fiber-optic capacity from Los Angeles to New York fell from $1.8 million in the first quarter of 2000 to $250,000 in 2003, and to $60,000 in late 2005. Rents for office space in San Francisco fell from $65.86 per square foot in 2000 to $28.75 in 2004.

The fiber stayed in the ground. Reliable, tested systems were in place to deal with every aspect of running an online business: payment systems and search engines, customer-relationship management software and logistics, data-mining and broadband service, storage and Web hosting. It all added up to a "fertile substrate that lets people experiment at very low cost," said Philip Rosedale, who founded the popular virtual world Second Life in 2003. In 2000, the costs of building his company would have been prohibitive. But Second Life's main overhead costs—a server grid of 2,000 CPUs, office space in San Francisco, Web hosting, data transmission—have all fallen sharply since then. "We are able to operate thousands of machines and use gigabytes of bandwidth, and it doesn't cost us very much," he says.

The dot-com prophets of the 1990s were right. Pervasive, cheap broadband would allow anyone with a good idea—or even a half-baked idea—and a little money to build business with global scale very quickly. And as the scandals multiplied and books like *New Yorker* scribe John Cassidy's *Dot.con* were commissioned and written, the audience of broadband users quickly began to catch up with the ambitions of entrepreneurs. An estimated 42 percent of Americans had high-speed Internet access at home in March 2006, according to the Pew Internet & American Life Project. That was up from 30 percent in 2005, an increase of 25 million users in twelve months. According to the FCC, the number of residential high-speed lines rose from 11 million in 2001 to 26 million in 2003 and to 43 million in December 2005.

The cheap technology and burgeoning user base meant that the world that George Gilder predicted was materializing—just too late for most of the companies whose stocks he promoted. But their failure spelled opportunity for others. Companies with better balance sheets who had weathered the storm picked up assets on the cheap. Level 3 Communications snapped up bankrupt broadband provider Genuity for about $60 million, and in 2005 bought up WilTel and a big chunk of bankrupt 360networks. Old media companies likewise bought Internet properties whose values had fallen precipitously. Dow Jones bought MarketWatch.com in November 2004, the New York Times bought About.com in March 2005, and NBC bought iVillage.com in March 2006.

The ability to transmit data, voice, and documents, to quickly upload and zap huge files through fat broadband pipes, contributed to a burst of innovation and growth among companies formed in the bubble or immediately afterward. Internet telephone companies like Vonage and Skype enlisted millions of customers; iTunes became a powerhouse in the music business. Infosys, India's largest technology outsourcing company, has seen its revenues more than triple since 2001. FreshDirect.com, an online grocer based in Queens, New York, founded in 2001, rang up $240 million in revenues in 2006. In the postbubble environment, Farrelly brothers companies became Ron Howard companies, the products of a beautiful mind. Enron and Blockbuster in 2000 engaged in an expensive and now-infamous trial of video-on-demand service, which yielded just seven purchases of *The Care Bears Movie* for $8.40. D'oh! Six years later, a dozen versions of content-over-broadband were thriving, and cable companies were ringing up huge profits selling DVR services and video on demand.

The spreading technology has altered not just business, but personal habits, lifestyle, popular culture, and politics.

In the late 1990s, it would have required an investment of a few thousand dollars and considerable technological skills to build and maintain a personal Web site. Today, it's possible to set up a blog for the price of a few movies. And because companies like Google and Blogads sell ad space in tiny bites, blogs have emerged as a small revenue source for thousands of self-obsessed writers, activists, and chroniclers of ephemera.

Many of the firms that have put the infrastructure to the best use are Old Economy companies that the dot-coms set out to kill. The online grocery store Peapod went public in 1997 and started flailing almost immediately. It was essentially sold for scrap in 2000 to Stop & Shop, which integrated the company's operations into its vast infrastructure. Now it's a real business. By 2003, Peapod was profitable in four of the five markets it served. In 2006, its trucks delivered groceries to 280,000 households up and down the Eastern seaboard. In one of those power-user households—mine—nearly as much money is spent on Peapod as is spent on health insurance premiums.

E-tailing didn't put bricks-and-mortar retailers out of business. But it has grown sufficiently to support real companies with real profit margins. U.S. online retail sales were an estimated $179 billion in 2005, and are growing at a 20 percent annual rate, according to Forrester Research. Many publications that relied exclusively on Internet advertising didn't survive the 1990s. But today, online ads are a reliable source of revenues for all media companies—old, new, and hybrid. The Interactive Advertising Bureau projected that online ad spending would rise from $12.5 billion in 2005 to $16 billion in 2006.

In this environment, social networking companies like Facebook, MySpace, and YouTube were able to gain massive scale for comparatively little investment. These companies may lose money, but not the way portals and start-up content firms did in the 1990s. Those pioneers devoured cash because they had huge budgets for marketing and creating proprietary content, and because ad dollars were hard to come by. The social networking sites, by contrast, spend virtually nothing on advertising and marketing, get virtually all of their content for free, courtesy of the users, and can tap into a growing stream of online advertising.

The list goes on, and publishing lead times being what they are, this will seem a little dated by the time it's printed. But it's clear that the excess capacity created in the 1990s has allowed entrepreneurs to build instant global brands and billion-dollar companies.

Is it a coincidence that the United States has been the center of Web 2.0? No. The cycle is an echo of the cycles that took place after the Internet and telegraph busts. According to the Organisation for Economic Co-operation and Development, the United States ranks just twelfth in the world for broadband penetration, behind Iceland, South Korea, and Japan, among others. But other nations haven't monetized their installed bases the way the United States has. The Internet is no longer exclusively an American phenomenon. And neither are the businesses surrounding it. Skype was created in 2003 by two Scandinavian dudes. But the value creation surrounding Web 2.0 has been disproportionately an American phenomenon. It is common to hear laments that India and China collectively graduate several times more engineers than the United States does. But quality counts, not quantity. The most significant engineering achievement in the last decade was achieved by the two guys from Stanford who founded Google.

Google, whose stock crossed $500 in November 2006, is in many ways the iconic company of the New New Era. It's a bandwidth hog that uses cheap broadband to great effect. It enjoys immense margins because most of its raw materials and business necessities are goods and services whose prices plummeted after the bust: storage and servers, engineers, software, and Bay Area office space. It services the new users who have embraced the Internet as a commercial platform—a gazillion businesses, large and small, paying for leads, clicks, listings, and search results. It sells and places online advertising. The content it provides is pretty much free, generated as it is by newspapers, companies, government agencies, and bloggers. And with the 2006 acquisition of YouTube, it became a consolidator.

So here we are, back where we started this inquiry. In the 1989 film *Crimes and Misdemeanors*, Lester, the obnoxious television producer played by Alan Alda, holds forth on how "comedy is tragedy plus time." In the dot-com space, the equation holds that tragedy + time = profits, innovation, and ultimately Google. And so it's possible to look back on the '90s and laugh now at the insanity, the pretensions, the willful self-delusion. But any postmortem would be incomplete without a consideration of the substantial benefits we continue to reap from the excess investment in Internet-related infrastructure.

For the profits and benefits extend far beyond Google's impressive market capitalization and lower bills for broadband access. In fact, there's a degree to which it is impossible to measure the true impact of the Internet on the American economy. As the promoters claimed in the 1990s, the Internet and the integration of information technology into businesses of all shapes and sizes has made them more responsive to changing economic conditions, more efficient, and more profitable. The ability of industries to outsource and manage supply chains, to make electronic payments, to customize products for customers, to communicate with suppliers effectively—all these developments have helped tame (but not eliminate) the business cycle and tamp down inflation. But it's exceedingly difficult to isolate the impact of the Internet, precisely because it is so fully integrated into our commercial lives.

Nowhere was the fantasy surrounding the Internet greater than in the United States. And nowhere has the technology been put to such useful economic and commercial effect. In the five years after 9/11, the United States added $2.36 trillion in annual gross domestic product. Every year, the United States creates an amount of new additional economic activity equal to the economy of South Korea. In the IMD Business School's annual ranking of global competitiveness, the United States remains number one, year in and year out, an astonishing achievement for a country of its size. The rest of the top ten, which includes Hong Kong, Singapore, Switzerland, and Luxembourg, have small populations or small geographical territories or small economies.

There are many ironies inherent in the boom-and-bust cycle. The Internet and the immense intellectual, physical, and virtual infrastructure erected in the 1990s have allowed companies to do more with less. Which means the spread of cheap Internet infrastructure, a huge boon to American consumers and to American companies, has not always been an unalloyed good for American workers. The excess capacity, the increased productivity, the ability to move work offshore—all these postboom developments contributed to slow job creation and a dampening of wage growth in the postbubble years. President George W. Bush's first term was the worst term for payroll job creation since that of Herbert Hoover; the number of payroll jobs actually fell 65,000 between January 2001 and January 2005. For five straight years, median wages stagnated.

What the dot-com and fiber-optic bubbles gave in the 1990s, in other words, they took away in the first years of the new century. And in the wake of the bust, job growth would have to rely on a bubble forming in a distinctly old economy industry: real estate.

6

REAL ESTATE

n the 1990s, dot-coms and fiber-optic companies were the economic analog to Miami Dolphins running back Ricky Williams—an inspired professional who carried the ball with flair, single-handedly powered the offense, and inspired comparisons to the all-time greats. Post-2001, those companies also turned out to be the economic analog to Williams—an erratic, pot-smoking slacker who left his supporters and promoters disappointed.

New Economy companies quickly slashed payrolls and capital investment budgets as they were revealed to be frauds, cheaters, and number fudgers. In a matter of weeks, Enron went from 20,000 employees to a few dozen, and WorldCom axed 60,000. Thomas Philippon of New York University and Simi Kedia of Rutgers Business School found that the hundreds of publicly held companies that restated earnings in 2000 and 2001, many of which were in the tech/fiber-optic/dot-com megaplex, cut between 250,000 and 600,000 jobs in 2001 and 2002. And the loss of high-paying jobs at WorldCom and Enron was only partially offset by the creation of jobs in the high-paying white-collar criminal defense sector.

While the economy-wide recession ended in November 2001, the domestic business investment recession deepened. "Real business fixed investment fell for nine consecutive quarters between the first quarter of 2001 and the first quarter of 2003," economist Brian Wesbury noted in the *Wall Street Journal*. "This was the worst period of decline in business investment since the data were first collected in 1947." The slowdown wasn't simply due to broken-down technology infrastructure builders. As globalization picked up pace, U.S. companies were more likely to outsource. Large companies like IBM and Dell either cut or simply added a few positions in the comparatively slow-growing domestic market; they hired with alacrity in comparatively fast-growing markets like India and China. Between 2001 and 2004, U.S. foreign direct investment outflows would rise from $142 billion to $224.1 billion. And so, middle managers who had fled Microsoft and General Electric in pursuit of dot-com wampum and casual dress codes often found the doors shut when they tried to return.

As a result, the United States lost payroll jobs for two more years after the recession ended. There were fewer private sector jobs in January 2005 than in January 2001, making George W. Bush the first president since Herbert Hoover to see payroll jobs decline in a full term. Of course, the job loss between 2000 and 2004 was nowhere near as gruesome as it had been between 1928 and 1932. And for that Bush could thank the rapid emergence of the Pop! dynamic in the housing and housing-related credit sectors.

Most of Bush's biblical allusions sailed far over the heads of the Washington press corps, which generally believes the New Testament is a spin-off of the *New Repub-lic*. But in a visit to the Gulf Coast in late August 2006, Bush used biblical language to sum up the positive impacts of the about-to-burst housing bubble. "And I suspect that what you'll see, Toby, is there will be a momentum, momentum will be gathered. Houses will begat jobs, jobs will begat houses." (And unto them option ARM mortgages shall be given. Verily, with resets and points few in number and monthly payments, lo into the third generation.)

A host of macroeconomic trends had spurred real es-tate in many markets to an enviable record in the 1990s. Between 1994 and 1999, for example, prices of existing homes rose by a healthy 4.4 percent annual rate, spurred by declining interest rates, the revival of cities from New York to San Francisco, graying baby boomers buying re-tirement homes, and broad economic growth. But starting in 2001 and 2002, the market took off like cyclist Floyd Landis on the seventeenth stage of the 2006 Tour de France. Once again, as with the prior Pop! cycles, a spreading sense that new rules were in effect and the mass willing sus-pension of disbelief led to an andrenaline-fueled spiral into mania.

It took something old, something new, and a lot of things borrowed to create the first twenty-first-century bubble. Land and real estate have always attracted sales-people, larger-than-life true believers, and borderline shy-sters with the ability to inspire others. Think of Howard

Roark of *The Fountainhead*, or Peter Gallagher's wolfish Buddy Kane the Real Estate King in *American Beauty*, or Donald Trump. The nation had started as something of a speculative land investment by greedy Europeans. Robert Morris, who almost single-handedly financed the American Revolution, amassed an empire of 8 million acres in western New York and Virginia in the 1790s but went bust. While the guys he had bankrolled were running the country, Morris languished in a debtors' prison for three years. And in the 1920s, the Florida real estate craze briefly captured the nation's attention before stocks got hot. But these were just proto-boomlets.

As in the 1920s, the Federal Reserve played a pivotal role in mixing up the suds. After the attacks of 9/11, Federal Reserve chairman Alan Greenspan sought to revive the shocked economy by furiously slashing the interest rate he controlled—the federal funds rate—from 3.5 percent to 1.75 percent in a matter of weeks. In June 2003, in the twilight of his central banking career, Greenspan lowered it to 1 percent and left it at the emergency level for a year. Meanwhile, other influential central bankers began to fret publicly about the prospects of deflation, which helped push long-term interest rates down. In November 2002, then-Federal Reserve governor Ben Bernanke warned that concern over deflation was "not purely hypothetical." Mortgage rates fell from about 8 percent in 2000 to about 6 percent in 2003.

Cheaper money—in some instances, near-free money—quickly found its way into the highly leveraged real estate industry. Existing home sales rose from 5.25 million in 2001 to 6.175 million in 2003, while the median price rose from $147,500 in 2001 to $178,800 in 2003, up 21 percent. New home starts bumped up from 1.6 million in 2001 to 1.85 million in 2003. And housing indeed begat jobs. If the United States was going to have a tidal wave of excess liquidity flowing into any sector, real estate was perhaps the best place to have it, from a nationalistic viewpoint. Building, selling, decorating, and renovating homes are labor-intensive endeavors. Each time a house is bought or built, a large and diverse crop of workers, blue-collar, white-collar, and no-collar, springs into action: mortgage brokers and lawyers, title insurers and deed recorders, appraisers and movers, architects and engineers, interior decorators and plumbers, hardware-store managers and Home Depot clerks, manufacturers of cement and lumber, chimney sweeps and home inspectors, septic-tank cleaners and landscapers, arborists and exterminators. Almost by definition, virtually all these jobs are domestic. Asha Bangalore, an economist at Northern Trust, found that between November 2001 and October 2005, housing and real estate accounted for 36 percent of U.S. private-sector payroll job growth, or 836,000 of 2.3 million.

Among the busiest bees were the growing legions of mortgage brokers and the mortgage bankers who bundled the loans they sold into securities. Here again, government policy played a key role. Banks were more than happy to extend credit to home buyers in part because they could sell many of them to Fannie Mae, a component of the New Deal–era financial infrastructure, and to its sibling, Freddie Mac. The two borrowed money from the public debt markets, bought mortgages from banks and lenders, and then either packaged them as securities or held them on their own balance sheet, so long as the loans conformed to their standards. As government-sponsored enterprises (GSEs), Fannie and Freddie are exempt from state and local income taxes and can borrow at favorable rates. (While Congress swears up and down that the federal government won't guarantee Fannie's and Freddie's debt, the market seems to think that when push comes to shove, the federal government will.) Economists Larry White and W. Scott Frame have concluded that thanks to the preferential treatment they receive in the markets, the two behemoths cause mortgage rates for conforming mortgages to be 20 to 25 basis points lower—i.e., 6.5 percent or 6.55 percent, instead of 6.75 percent. The Congressional Budget Office found that the GSEs in 2003 thus saved borrowers $13.4 billion.

In fact, it appears that Fannie and Freddie were designed to be bubble enablers. The size of the mortgages they buy (and whose credit quality they ensure) is tied to the rise in average home prices, not to inflation. The more house prices rise, the more Fannie Mae is willing to lend.

The limit rose every year between 1992 and 2006, and soared from $252,700 in 2000 to $322,700 in 2003, an increase of 27.7 percent; in the next three years the limit would rise another 29 percent, to $417,000. Despite a series of scandals and fitful congressional efforts to rein in the growth of the mortgage giants, Fannie Mae and Freddie Mac spread credit around liberally.

Loans that conformed to the standards of Fannie Mae and Freddie Mac were only part of the lending universe. The GSEs don't buy mortgages above the limit, which puts vast tracts of the Northeast and the West Coast beyond their purview. The private sector followed the GSEs' lead in providing capital liberally. Subprime loans—high-interest loans to people with poor credit—are the mortgage equivalent of high-yield bonds. In 2000, subprime lending was a niche industry, with just 719,000 loans outstanding representing about 2.4 percent of all mortgages. But the business gained scale on the infrastructure platform created during two previous Pop! cycles. Banks and mortgage companies could borrow money cheaply, make loans at high rates, and then sell the loans into the vast mortgage-backed securities market that Fannie Mae had pioneered. The Internet became a tremendous platform for pitching housing-related finance. LendingTree.com and Bankrate.com served as dating sites for eager borrowers and eager lenders willing to offer the credit version of online sex: instant credit approval. E-mail inboxes began to overflow with mortgage-related spam, and much of the burgeoning online ad business consisted of refinancing offers. Subprime originations, $210 billion in 2001, rose to $350 billion in 2003 and $625 billion in 2005.

Increasingly, the loans extended were not plain vanilla thirty-year fixed mortgages. And here, too, the Federal Reserve played a key role in encouraging mortgage innovation. As housing became more expensive, lenders began to offer adjustable rate mortgages, which let borrowers keep payment costs down for the first few years with a teaser rate. In exchange, homeowners assumed the risk that interest rates would be higher when the rates would readjust to market-pegged rates in a year or three years or five years. The teaser rates pivoted off interest rates on short-term government bonds, which were most heavily influenced by the Fed's policies. What's more, the Fed sent out clear messages that ARMs were not dangerous. If deflation was a fear—as Ben Bernanke had intimated—then borrowers didn't have to worry about rates getting reset markedly higher in the near future. On February 27, 2004, Fed chairman Alan Greenspan, speaking before the Credit Union National Association, explained that, given the recent history of falling rates, choosing an ARM, with its lower short-term rate, was a no-brainer. ARMs rose from 12 percent of mortgages sold in 2001 to 19 percent in 2003.

Low interest rates spurred housing and the credit industry in three different ways. In markets where supply and land were constrained, on the coasts and in cities, cheaper credit meant people could afford to pay more for the same apartments and houses. So prices spiked. In the Northeast between 2003 and 2005, existing home prices rose 29.2 percent. In areas where land was plentiful, like Phoenix and Las Vegas, cheap money was plowed into new communities, subdivisions, and condos. Between 2002 and 2005, housing rose 21 percent. And everywhere, the boom played out in rising mortgage and mortgage-related debt.

In all instances, growth was fueled by groups of eager promoters: real estate brokers and mortgage brokers. These hot new professions had few barriers to entry—a phone, an e-mail account, some rudimentary training, and you were in business—and offered quick riches. Between 1998 and 2006, the number of real estate agents rose from 718,000 to 1.37 million, and the number of people employed by mortgage brokers soared from 240,000 in 2000 to 418,700 in 2004. The industry began to impose itself on the culture, just as dot-coms had in the 1990s. Points, HELOCs (home equity lines of credit), and re-fi replaced eyeballs, URLs, and EBITDA in the commercial vernacular. The frenzied ads for E*Trade were replaced by comforting messages from mortgage companies: "When your bank says no, Champion says yes." At Argent, an upstart subprime lender based in Irvine, California, the vibe circa 2005 was Silicon Valley South. The company sponsored Danica Patrick, the brash woman race car driver. And the business-casual-every-day headquarters expanded so rapidly that veteran employees easily got lost and confused.

David Lereah, chief economist at the National Association of Realtors, was thrust forward in the role of a present-day George Gilder or Irving Fisher. Every month, he had the happy task of going on CNBC and crowing about the latest numbers on housing starts and housing prices. Fueled in part by Lereah, the narrative told about housing began to change. The French word for real estate may be *immobilier*. But homes were no longer solid, unmoving assets. They weren't simply places to sit in an enormous chair and eat chocolate. They were investments. In February 2005, Lereah published *Are You Missing the Real Estate Boom? Why Home Values and Other Real Estate Investments Will Climb Through the End of the Decade—and How to Profit from Them*. (It didn't win a National Book Award, but it did win the prize for Longest Nonacademic Book Title of 2005.) Real estate, now in the midst of a permanent boom, fueled by demographics and the changes in the marketing and financing of homes, represented a "once-in-every-other-generation opportunity."

Of course, this argument required the sort of willful forgetting of history that happens in every bubble. Robert Shiller, the author of *Irrational Exuberance*, liked to point out that in real terms, residential housing in the United States rose 66 percent from 1890 to 2004, or just 0.4 percent a year. But such observations had the same effect as the fuddy-duddy stock analysts who claimed that publicly held stocks should report actual earnings in 1998. Housing was putting up excellent numbers in the new century. Like tech stocks in the 1990s, homes and the securities related to them morphed into an asset class that belonged in everyone's portfolio that could be—no, must be—bought at any price, risk free and on margin.

Here, again, government policy played an important enabling role. Economist Jason Furman argued in *Slate* that in 2005 the government provided some $200 billion in subsidies for housing. The largest subsidy was the mortgage interest deduction. Introduced along with the income tax in 1913, it wasn't widely used until the 1950s, when home ownership soared. Individuals today are able to deduct interest on up to $1 million in mortgage indebtedness on two homes, plus interest on another $100,000 in home equity loans. During the boom years, deductions soared to nearly $70 billion in 2003. Cleveland State University Cleveland-Marshall College of Law professor Deborah Geier concluded that the home mortgage deduction is the third-largest single "tax expenditure" behind the deductions companies take for contributions to pension plans and for health-care premiums.

Roger Lowenstein, writing in the *New York Times Magazine* in March 2006, argued that the deduction didn't boost home ownership rates. More than 70 percent of tax filers don't get any benefit from the deduction because they don't itemize their deductions. "In normal times, the deduction may not make the difference for most borrowers," he wrote. But these were no longer normal times. In fact, the deduction was nicely designed to promote investment and speculation in the new century. The rise of a class of mass affluents—in 2004, 19.7 million households made more than $100,000—meant there were more itemizers each year. As home prices rose, interest payments grew, and so did the value of the deduction. It entered the calculation for more home buyers, and especially for those who bought second homes as investments. The ability to deduct interest provides the most bang for the buck in the first year of a mortgage. Buy a $333,000 condo with $33,000 down and a 6 percent interest-only mortgage. In the first year, the investor pays $18,000 in interest ($12,000 after taxes). A year later, the price rises by 11 percent. The condo is sold for $370,000, the investor nets a 55 percent return on the cash invested.

Other components of the tax code acted as public subsidies for speculative home investors. People selling their primary residences are allowed to shield up to $500,000 in capital gains from a home sale. And under Section 1031 of the U.S. Internal Revenue Code, people who sell investment properties can defer capital gains by rolling the cash into a new investment property within 180 days. This benefit, with its short half-life, provides incentives for people who cash in not to diversify, but to put the currency quickly back to work in the same asset class. Add it all up—the incentives favoring borrowing, the infrastructure guaranteeing the purchase of the debt, the Fed handing out free money and encouraging people to take ARMs—and the private sector didn't need a promoter to encourage people to take the plunge.

Housing begat jobs and jobs begat housing. Nationwide, home prices rose 9.3 percent in 2004 and 12.4 percent in 2005. Combined new and existing home sales in 2005 were 8.357 million, up from 6.7 million in 2000. In 2005, when a record 8 percent of the housing stock turned over, single family starts rose to 1.75 million, up from 1.25 million in 2000. And as the sector grew, it swelled to dominate the economy. In mid-2004, gross private residential domestic investment surpassed consumer spending on goods. In submarkets, such as Vero Beach, Florida, real estate and housing accounted for nearly 20 percent of jobs in early 2005. Housing soared from 3.5 percent of gross domestic product in 1990 to an all-time peak of 6.2 percent in the first quarter of 2006.

Never before had housing occupied such a central role in the nation's economy. For in addition to creating jobs, housing and housing-related credit emerged rapidly as a source of spending money. During the housing bubble years, real wages stagnated: between 2000 and 2005, median earnings fell after accounting for inflation. But Americans needed cash to carry out their most deeply cherished civic duty: shopping. In the absence of raises and bonuses, consumers increasingly looked to their homes for "income." Home equity lines of credit swelled from $420.7 billion in the first quarter of 2000 to $714.8 billion in the first quarter of 2004, and $917.25 billion in the first quarter of 2005. Between HELOCs, gains from selling inflated homes, and the growing phenomenon of cash-out refinancings, so-called mortgage equity withdrawal (MEW) became a significant factor. Alan Greenspan and Mark Kennedy, a colleague at the Federal Reserve, determined that MEW rose from $59.1 billion in the fourth quarter of 2001, or 3.14 percent of disposable income, to $206.7 billion in the third quarter of 2004, or 9.5 percent of disposable income.

By 2005, the classic signs of a bubble were evident. The accumulated decades of bitter experience and wisdom were discarded. In the fall of 2005, Miami real estate broker Mark Zilbert launched Condoflip.com, a Web site where hotshots could flip $600,000 preconstruction condos in Miami the way day traders flip $6 stocks. The company's insouciant slogan: "Bubbles are for bathtubs." Meanwhile, investors had already been flipping housing stocks with abandon. The chart of the S&P Homebuilders index, which soared from 201.34 in September 2001 to 1,323 in July 2005, looked a lot like the chart of RCA in the 1920s. Publicly held home builders drove the soaring bull market sleigh: on, Pulte; on, Beazer; on, Toll; on, Lennar! The business best-seller list was stocked by tomes preaching the virtue of home investment. According to the National Association of Realtors, in 2005, 28 percent of homes were bought as investments. In Ocean City, New Jersey, 75 percent of the mortgage originations in the 2005 third quarter were written to investors.

As in previous booms, there were some skeptics. Housing Bubble and the Housing Bubble blog went live in January 2004 and April 2005, respectively. James Grant of *Grant's Interest Rate Observer* had a field day pointing out some of the absurdities of the lending business, cheekily posting charts that looked like hockey sticks—steady or stable patterns resolving with sharp upswings to the right in the post-2002 period. David Rosenberg, North American economist at Merrill, Lynch, in March 2005 constructed twin charts showing that household real estate assets had hit 140 percent of gross domestic product, the precise ratio that household mutual fund and stock assets had hit in 2000, just before the peak. Bubble-ologist Robert Shiller and Wellesley College professor Karl Case developed futures contracts based on home price indices in hot markets, which would offer pessimists the ability to buy puts on Las Vegas.

But the plaintive warnings were easily drowned out as housing crossed the thin line separating an investment craze from a popular culture phenomenon. Miami condo promoters became the new dot-coms, known for outrageous, expensive, hype-filled parties. Abby Goodnough of the *New York Times* described the May 2005 scene in Miami, a city with a population of 400,000 people and 70,000 condos in the works. The launch party for 360-unit Paramount Bay featured models hanging out and then-*View* gabber Star Jones interviewing the architect. A launch for a project dubbed Cynergi sounded like a hellish amalgamation of an after-hours club and the birthday party of a spoiled three-year-old: "a drag queen D.J., macaroni and cheese, inflatable lounge chairs and a blank canvas for guests to paint on." On television, Carmela Soprano, at long last asserting her independence and planning for a post-Tony future, started building a huge spec house. Channel flippers in the summer of 2005 could tune into reality shows like *Flip This House*, on the A&E network, and *Flip That House*, on the Learning Channel. October brought the debut of the inevitable real estate sitcom, inevitably titled *Hot Properties*, and inevitably detailing the escapades of four hot female brokers.

Every bubble needs a prominent magazine cover to call its top. This time, the *New York Times Magazine* supplied it, with Robert Toll, the founder of McMansion manufacturer Toll Brothers, in the role of John J. Raskob. In the October 16, 2005, issue, Toll made his case, which was eerily reminiscent of the case made for buying stocks on margin in the fall of 1929. A new era had dawned, he told writer Jon Gertner, and trends of the recent years could be extrapolated endlessly into the future. Toll foresaw a brave new world in which high-income folks would soon pay half their incomes for mortgages, and in which an average million-dollar suburban home would go for $4 million. Toll would brook no dissent. "The company expects to grow by 20 percent for the next two years and then will strive for 15 percent annually after that," he said.

Toll could be forgiven for thinking that American home buyers would prove endlessly Kennedyesque, willing to pay any price, bear any burden for that 4,000-square-foot center-hall Tuscan colonial with double-height foyer, heated terrazzo-tile bathrooms, and libraries uncluttered with books. For in the parts of the country where Toll operated, affordable housing had become something of an oxymoron. For several years running, housing prices had far outstripped income gains. Nationwide, mortgage payments on median-priced homes ate up about 20 percent of income in 2005, according to Goldman, Sachs. But in Los Angeles, the ratio had risen from about 30 percent in 1999 to 50 percent in 2005, and in New York from 25 percent in 1999 to about 40 percent in 2005. The ratio of median home price to household income rose from 3.3 in 2000 to 4.8 in 2005. When Mark Zandi of Economy.com created price-to-earnings ratios for housing (the rent a house could expect to bring in divided into its price), he found that the national P/E had risen from 9.3 in 2000 to 15 in 2005. In Las Vegas and West Palm Beach, the ratios were 121.3 and 120, respectively.

The housing credit bubble helped prolong the housing bubble, for when prices rose, home buyers didn't bargain. They borrowed more, put less money down, extended payment periods, and assumed long-term mortgages. Thirty-year, plain vanilla fixed mortgages became relics of the 1960s, like the plain vanilla musical act Sha Na Na. New classes of products, conjured into existence by mortgage companies, staked out huge chunks of the market. In November 2005, Ownit Mortgage Solutions introduced a forty-five-year mortgage. And mortgage brokers increasingly dealt funky loans: subprime and alt-a loans (loans with incomplete documentation), ARMs and interest-only mortgages, and option ARMs. If mortgage debt was an addictive drug, option ARMs—known by the street name negative amortization loans—were crack crystals. Neg am loans give buyers the option of paying the interest, or of not paying the monthly interest bill and seeing their debt rise. (In the meantime, lenders book the unpaid interest as cash earnings.) According to UBS, interest-only mortgages, option ARMs, and other so-called affordability loans accounted for 25 percent of the mortgage dollars lent in 2004 and 2005. Combined, subprime and alt-a loans swelled to a $1.2 trillion market by the summer of 2005. In the first half of 2006, option ARMs were 15 percent of originations, compared to 8 percent in the first half of 2005.

Increasingly, these loans were supplied not by the descendants of friendly local mortgage banker George Bailey, but by less-regulated or unregulated financial firms. In search of high returns, mortgage REITs, investment banks, hedge funds, and private equity firms all began feverishly to put money to work in the riskiest part of the housing sector. "American Home Mortgage Investment Corp., for instance, originated about $5.4 billion of option ARMs in the third quarter of 2006, making it the no. 7 option ARM lender," *BusinessWeek* reported. Hmm. Unregulated newbies getting into the lending on speculative assets late in a cycle? It was like Standard Oil getting into the call market in 1929. And just as happened in the 1920s, snobby Wall Street firms began to invest in formerly déclassé businesses. In August 2006, Morgan Stanley, a descendant of J. P. Morgan's original firm, bought subprime lender Saxon Capital.

Lending expanded at such a furious pace that it seemed as if the industry had experienced a mass lobotomy in which the lobe that can account for the possibility of rising interest rates, inflation, and declining asset prices had been removed. "Why can't real estate just have a boom like every other industry?" Robert Toll wondered. "Why do we have to have a bubble and then pop?"

Toll clearly hadn't read the proposal for this book or dipped a toe into the deep pool of bubble literature. For despite the promises of a new era, as happens every time, the oldest laws of economics still applied to the housing and housing credit markets. One by one, starting at about the time Toll's visage peered out from the cover of the *New York Times Magazine*, the assumptions underlying the bubble deflated. Interest rates turned out to be cyclical after all, especially for those borrowing short-term. The Federal Reserve, ending the era of cheap money that started in June 2004, took the federal funds rate from 1 percent to 5.25 percent over two years, which made short-term money more expensive. While the increases didn't have much effect on fixed-rate long-term mortgages, they had a significant effect on the huge volume of ARMs of recent vintage. All those loans taken out in 2003 and 2004 that were due to reset in 2005 and 2006 would reset at much higher rates.

Meanwhile, a classic disconnect between supply and demand had opened up. It wasn't quite Global Crossing and its competitors building two generations' worth of fiber-optic cable in a few years. But there was too much building and too many homes for sale. In the fall of 2006, 28,258 new condo units were either under construction or being planned in Manhattan; for all of 2005, sales of new condos had totaled 4,000. By the summer of 2006, nearly 4 million homes were for sale in the United States, nearly double the inventory of 2000. In some markets, the mismatch was tragic. In Palm Beach County, Florida, reported hedge fund manager Doug Kass, there were 12,121 housing units for sale in September 2006, and only 304 had sold in the month—that's forty months of inventory.

The cracks appeared first in the fall of 2005, with reports that monthly sales volumes and prices were falling. In July 2006, home prices showed their first year-over-year decline in eleven years. Next, the publicly held home builders began to slash their earnings estimates, confidently calling a bottom each time, only to lower earnings again several weeks later. Toll Brothers, whose stock peaked in July 2006 at 57, having run up nearly eight times since September 2001, fell to 30 in the spring of 2006. In 2006, instead of rising 15 percent, as Robert Toll had blithely projected, the number of homes Toll Brothers delivered fell 3.5 percent. In December 2006, the company projected 2007 deliveries would be up to 30 percent *lower* than the 2005 total. The XHB, an exchanged-traded fund on the S&P 500 Homebuilders index introduced in February 2006, lost 35 percent in its first five months of trading.

Housing had lost its mojo. Rather than acting as a source of jobs, housing was now shedding jobs. Instead of a spur to consumer spending and hence the economy, housing became a drag—a key factor in the sharply slowing rate of growth in mid-2006. Carmela Soprano's spec house stood, unfinished and unsold. Forced to come up with optimistic quotes to accompany the monthly housing reports, David Lereah began to channel Baghdad Bob. "This may be the bottom," he said in May 2006. "It appears we've hit bottom, the price drops are necessary to stir sales," he said in December 2006. On July 20, Ben Bernanke told Congress,

"The downturn in the housing market so far appears to be orderly."

In the subprime market, which in June 2006 totaled 5.7 million loans, or 13.4 percent of the total, the downturn was far from orderly. By June 2006, 6.2 percent of subprime loans were in foreclosure or arrears. Excess investment in subprime lenders led to a fire sale. When Champion's parent company, KeyCorp, put it up for sale in the fall of 2006, buyers just said no. The subprime mortgage operation sold for $130 million, nearly half the anticipated price. Ownit .com, the purveyor of the forty-five-year mortgage and one of the fifteen largest subprime lenders, simply closed up shop. There were other classic postbubble-piercing events. Pinnacle, an Atlanta-based company that advertised in *Newsweek* and other national publications, promising returns of 25 percent in sixty days with a minimum investment of $5,000 by investing in foreclosed homes, was revealed to be little more than a Ponzi scheme.

Nationwide, home prices fell 3.1 percent between November 2005 and November 2006. That doesn't sound like much, especially compared with the massive carnage in NASDAQ stocks a few years earlier. But the situation was more reminiscent of 1929. Houses—especially investment properties—were like expensive stocks bought on margin, with little money down. In the fall of 2006, Christopher Cagan, an analyst with First American Real Estate Solutions, calculated that owners of 29 percent of the homes that closed in the first nine months of 2005 were sitting on zero or negative equity.

And so the buying frenzy shifted quickly to a selling frenzy. By the fall of 2006, Condoflip.com featured three panic buttons. A seller pushing the red button, level 3, agreed to forfeit half the deposit in exchange for being released from the commitment to buy a condo. As prices fell and the market became gripped by what D. R. Horton CEO Don Tomnitz dubbed "bad psychology," buyers walked away from deposits rather than getting saddled with highly leveraged depreciating assets. David Rosenberg of Merrill, Lynch noted that in the third quarter of 2006, 42 percent of the buyers of new homes cancelled their contracts.

As Carson Daly rang in the New Year, the twin housing and credit bubbles were still unraveling. Given that, it may be too early to total up the macroeconomic losses and gains. But for those able to look on the bright side of the darkest cloud, the upsides of the bubble are already apparent. The bubble achieved a goal that billions of federal dollars, and thirty years of good intentions, could not: gentrification and renewal in some of the formerly most wretched spots of cities. The South Bronx, burning in the 1970s, has become the new Williamsburg, a haven for artists and hipsters and a magnet for private capital. Indeed, with each passing week, the *New York Times* "Living In" column introduced its bourgeois readers to newly acceptable 'hoods: Washington Heights and East Harlem in Manhattan,

Ditmas Park in Brooklyn. *New York* magazine's perpetual search for the next hot neighborhood ultimately led it to Jersey City. And in its wisdom, the market rewarded urban pioneers, not the yuppies who followed them. People who bought derelict properties from the city in marginal neighborhoods in the 1990s made out like bandits. Lovelynn Gwinn, profiled in the *New York Times*, bought a house on West 138th Street, near Riverside Drive, for less than $250,000 in 2000 and put it on the market for $1.4 million in 2006.

The bubble also led to some much-needed internal distribution of population. Thanks to Internet services like Realtor.com, it became possible for homeowners to learn how far their housing dollars could go in other areas. For those in the New York area, one of the most distressing online activities in recent years has been to punch in a random zip code in Montana or Wisconsin and imagine how much happier you might be with 5,000 square feet instead of 2,300 (and how miserable you'd be without access to Vietnamese takeout). In 2004, as Motoko Rich and David Leonhardt reported in the *New York Times*, some 500,000 people, many of them fed up with high housing prices, left California for cheaper housing markets like Utah, Nevada, and Missouri. "They just walk in and go, 'Wow, we can have space,'" Kansas City real estate broker Sandy Tasker said of the reverse Joads. In 2004, 2,200 people moved from California to Missouri, more than three times the number who made the trek in 2001. In 2004 New York suffered a net loss of 11,500 citizens to Philadelphia, of all places.

As with the fiber-optic/dot-com boom, the housing/housing-credit boom has left behind a twofold infrastructure. First, there's the physical infrastructure. Broadly speaking, America's housing stock has been upgraded, with new construction and renovation in every corner of the market. And the excess capacity in real estate will be marked down and sold (some of it at catastrophic losses) but not torn down. Some developers in south Florida might go bankrupt, but their half-finished condo towers will be completed and turned into hotels or office buildings or dormitories for rich kids at the University of Miami.

It's also possible at this early date to discern the outlines of a new mental infrastructure. During the bubble, Americans—for all the mistakes they surely have made—became more sophisticated about home finance. In the third quarter of 2006, a record 69 percent of Americans owned homes, compared with 66.8 percent in 1999. With each passing year, more people thus became attuned to the benefits of owning rather than renting, and of borrowing against home equity at 8 percent (plus a taxpayer subsidy) instead of borrowing on credit cards at 20 percent. Ten years ago, only bond traders watched the movement of interest rates and tried to profit from them. Today, tens of millions of homeowners do. For all the unfortunates who took on adjustable-rate mortgages at exactly the wrong time (thanks for the advice, Chairman Al), many others were quite smart—refinancing again and again. This knowledge and experience has now become embedded in the culture and practice of personal finance.

We also get to keep the services introduced in the bubble, like Domania.com, the site that lets snoopers learn how much their neighbors paid for their house in 1999, or Zillow.com, which uses algorithms and sales data to spit out estimated market values. Indeed, the greater sense of transparency and the greater availability of information about all components of the home sales process—mortgages and listings, past purchase prices and regional market data—are clearly an unalloyed good for the consumer.

Finally, excess capacity generally spurs price wars, which is always good for the mass of consumers. With volume slowing and prices falling, the balance of power between real estate agents and their clients has clearly shifted. During the bubble, the agent's commission, 5 percent or 6 percent in most markets, was unassailable. In 2005, people who insisted on paying only a 4.5 percent commission for listing a house would have been told to stuff it. In 2007, people who insist on paying only a 4.5 percent commission for listing a house will find plenty of brokers willing to return their calls.

Peering ahead, it's possible that a new and beneficial spreading of risk could take root from the wreckage of the housing bubble, much as a new and beneficial spreading of risk took root in the early 1930s. In 2006, the housing index options traded on the Chicago Board of Trade were still a small and liquid market. But people tend to see the necessity for insurance and hedging only after the fall. People insure their homes against loss due to fire and floods in part because lenders require them to, and because it's a way of socializing risk. What if lenders offered lower interest rates or better payment terms to people who bought insurance against downturns in their local housing market? Stranger things have happened.

Regardless of its long-term impact, the housing and real estate bubble served as an important catalyst for growth at a time when one was sorely needed. In 2006, it seemed to have successfully passed the torch of leadership to other sectors of the economy. One sector in particular would provide a source of alternative energy.

7

ALTERNATIVE
ENERGY

The July 2006 Fortune/Aspen Institute Brainstorm featured more A-listers than the *Vanity Fair* Oscars party. Queen Noor of Jordan discussed the Middle East conflict; Ayaan Hirsi Ali, the former Dutch parliamentarian, warned against the spread of Islamic extremism; Sears chairman Eddie Lampert held forth on corporate responsibility; and cycling deity Lance Armstrong graced a panel on cancer research. One of the most heavily attended sessions featured Silicon Valley aristocrat Vinod Khosla, a cofounder of Sun Microsystems and a longtime partner at Kleiner, Perkins, Caufield & Byers, the venture capital firm that backed Amazon.com, Google, and Excite. Arriving a few minutes late, I pulled up a bench outside the packed conference room as rain clouds momentarily blackened the sky. I scooted over to make room for an older woman, who craned her neck, in part to hear the soft-spoken Khosla, in part to avoid the drizzling rain. None of the khaki-clad type-As inside bothered to give up his seat for retired Supreme Court justice Sandra Day O'Connor.

Khosla wasn't talking about the latest Web 3.0 social network peer-to-peer scalable business. Rather, in a quiet measured voice, he was discussing the relative virtues of ethanol derived from cellulose (plants like switchgrass) and ethanol derived from corn. Khosla, who set up his own venture firm in 2004, had just set up a new company, Cilion, with grain-milling giant Western Milling, to build and operate ethanol refining plants. He was also backing a California ballot initiative that would tax oil companies to generate $4 billion to fund alternative energy projects. So long as oil remained above $40 a barrel, Khosla argued, ethanol remained a viable alternative. And with each passing month, as more flex-fuel cars were produced, the investment opportunity was growing more attractive. "Innovation is the cessation of stupidity," he said.

Alternative energy, renewable fuels, energy efficiency, and climate changes were hot topics at the Fortune Brainstorm, which, as had become chic at gatherings of the bienpensant, was carbon neutral. And Khosla was a member of the elite group of bubble surfers who survived the dot-com wipeout, got back up on their boards, and began hanging ten on the new wave: alternative energy. Excite@Home's fancy headquarters was still largely empty, but thunder was once again emanating from Silicon Valley, peals of impenetrable engineer-speak and soaring save-the-world rhetoric. With the volume of flattering media coverage and hot IPOs rising, venture capitalists were stampeding like a herd of wildebeest, and conservative corporations were glomming on to a progressive cause with the zeal of the converted.

In the 1970s, the oil crisis had sparked interest and investment in solar energy and biofuels. In 1975, renewable energy accounted for 7.7 percent of the U.S. supply.

Hydroelectricity, generated by dams built in the 1930s, another enduring piece of New Deal commercial infrastructure, accounted for more than half the total. But the enthusiasm dissipated once oil prices subsided. By 2001, renewable energy accounted for just 7.4 percent of energy supply. In the fevered months after 9/11, however, interest in alternative energy rose sharply. The U.S. invasion of Iraq, the rise of Hugo Chávez in Venezuela, and the industrialization of China and India heightened concerns over the viability and stability of global oil supplies. Hubbert's peak, the half-century-old argument by geophysicist Marion King Hubbert that oil prices would spike as peak production neared, took its place alongside Moore's law as a business buzzword. Matthew Simmons, one of the few analysts to have called bullshit on Enron in the 1990s, argued in his 2005 book, *Twilight in the Desert*, that Saudi Arabia was running out of oil.

As oil breached the $60 per barrel barrier, analysts began to extrapolate. In late 2005, investment manager Felix Zulauf, a member of the *Barron's* annual roundtable, projected that oil would rise to $100 per barrel this decade. As wildflowers sprouted in the Alps in December and white Christmas in New England became a fond memory, executives began to speak about a carbon-constrained environment. In virtually every seat of power, save the White House and the offices of Senator James Inhofe of Oklahoma, brows furrowed deeply about emissions and climate change. Green prophets, like Amory Lovins, head of the Rocky Mountain Institute, became fixtures on the *Charlie Rose* show. In the space of a few years, alternative energy evolved from the province of tinkerers, geeks, and Birkenstock-wearing tree huggers to a mainstream phenomenon. A robust masala of renewed enthusiasm for renewable energy was simmering.

Once again, experts began talking about a New Era for a crucial industry, in which old rules no longer applied. This time, it was a new geopolitical era. As the involvement in Iraq stretched beyond the duration of World War II and domestic supplies dwindled to a comparative trickle, Americans came to realize that their addiction to imported oil had a higher cost than the dollars spent at the pump. "We wouldn't normally think of a light bulb as an instrument for security, but building real security can be as simple and as grassroots-based as a compact fluorescent bulb," Amory Lovins wrote in 2002. "Long-term security and economic prosperity requires the creation of a fourth pillar—technological transformation of the transportation sector through what might be called 'fuel choice,' " reads the manifesto of Set America Free, a coalition of neoconservative neoconservationists whose ranks included foreign policy analysts Daniel Pipes and Frank Gaffney. "By leading multinational efforts rooted in the following principles, the United States can *immediately* begin to introduce a global economy based on next-generation fuels and vehicles that can utilize them." The need to pursue alternate supplies of energy became one of the few things that steak tartare–eating Vulcans and hemp-wearing vegans could agree upon.

Ethanol was the most visible manifestation of the emerging boom. A cottage industry in the 1980s, it grew to production of 870 million gallons in 1989, or 0.8 percent of gasoline consumption that year. After 9/11, production took flight, rising 20 percent in 2002 and 27 percent in 2003. By 2005, when the United States overtook Brazil as the Saudi Arabia of ethanol, production reached 3.9 billion gallons, nearly twice the 2001 total and accounting for 2.8 percent of gasoline involved in transport.

The ethanol industry is—and always has been—massively subsidized by the federal government. Federal support for grow-your-own gasoline is the rare issue that unites committed internationalists and xenophobes and, given the continuing prominence of the Iowa caucus, Democratic and Republican presidential candidates. For the last quarter century, the federal government has offered a tax credit of at least $0.50 per gallon to companies that refine and blend ethanol into gasoline. (Today, it stands at $0.51 per gallon.) With production of 3.9 billion gallons in 2005, that amounted to a $1.99 billion subsidy. Meanwhile, the United States stubbornly maintains a $0.54-per-gallon protective tarriff on sugar-based ethanol produced by Brazil. The Energy Policy Act of 2005, signed in August 2005, gave a further federal boost to the industry by mandating that production rise from 4 billion gallons in 2006 to 7.5 billion gallons by 2012. Meanwhile, state efforts to ban the use of MTBE (methyl tertiary-butyl ether), an oxygenate blended into gasoline that polluted water sources, have also encouraged the greater use of ethanol, the only commercially available substitute for MTBE.

The U.S. ethanol industry has long been dominated by Archer Daniels Midland (ADM), the massive grain processor (fiscal 2006 sales: $36.6 billion). ADM, which used to call itself the "Supermarket to the World," quickly evolved into the ExxonMobil of ethanol. It owns about one-quarter of the nation's ethanol production capacity. And in April 2006, ADM hired the former head of Chevron's refining business, Patricia Woertz, as its new chief executive officer. Citigroup analyst David Driscoll told the *New York Times* that ADM would likely earn $1.3 billion from ethanol in fiscal 2007.

Plenty of start-ups were eager to challenge ADM. And given the huge safety net provided by federal subsidies, and the high price of oil, Wall Street bankers and private equity sharpies began landing in fly-over country. Hawkeye Renewables, founded in 2003, raised cash to build two large refineries in Iowa. In November 2005, Bill Gates's private investment vehicle took an $84 million stake in Pacific Ethanol. In June 2006, ethanol companies VeraSun Energy and Aventine Renewable raised $420 million and $391 million in initial public offerings, respectively. US BioEnergy, a

South Dakota firm founded in 2004, staged a $150 million IPO in December 2006. Private equity investments in biofuels in the United States rose from near zero in the first five months of 2005 to nearly a billion in the first five months of 2006. "Wall Street is drunk on ethanol," James Mackintosh of the *Financial Times* reported in June 2006, "pouring cash into constructing refineries and searching for any company that can claim a link to 'green' fuel."

Much of the capital went straight into infrastructure. Between January 2002 and January 2006, the nation's ethanol manufacturing capacity nearly doubled, from 2.34 billion gallons per year to 4.34 billion gallons per year. In January 2006, there were thirty-one plants under construction with 1.8 billion gallons of capacity. By 2008, if all the plants planned at the end of 2006 are built, capacity will soar to nearly 10.7 billion gallons.

As in other booms, the flood of cash and enthusiasm inflated the price of vital commodities. The price of a contract for the delivery of a bushel of corn in December 2006 on the Chicago Board of Trade (one of the businesses that the telegraph helped conjure into existence) rose dramatically in 2006, from about $2.50 to $3.50. Ethanol futures began to trade on the CBOT in May 2006. And as the price of corn became a proxy for ethanol production, the volume of corn contracts traded rose 142 percent between November 2005 and November 2006. Protein producers—

industrial-scale pork, beef, and chicken growers—began to report lower profits due to the rising cost of a key input.

Just as the railroad had opened up the empty Great Plains for development in the 1870s, the emerging ethanol boom now promises to open up the emptying Great Plains for development. High house prices may have spurred Californians to move to Kansas City, but even the prospect of $2 million, 1,800-square-foot ranch homes in Encino would not have spurred an exodus to the frigid, sparsely populated Dakotas. But the prospect of corn being turned into a liquid fuel has warmed the hearts of farmers, long accustomed to seeing their children move away for better jobs. Analyst Joel Kotkin noted that ethanol was helping to fuel a long-awaited economic revival in the Badlands. "We're on the verge of a gold rush driven by energy," said Bob Valeu, state coordinator for North Dakota senator Byron Dorgan. Increasingly, the economic development strategy for huge chunks of the nation revolved around building ethanol plants. In River City, the band could be sponsored by the local ethanol company!

Skeptics hastened to point out inconvenient economic and scientific truths. A plant that produces 100 million gallons per year of ethanol would chow enough corn to feed half a million head of cattle. If all the plants under construction were to operate at full capacity, they'd devour ever-larger chunks of the corn crop. The U.S. Department of

Agriculture estimated that 14 percent of the 2005 bumper crop of 10.55 billion bushels was used for ethanol, up from 11 percent in 2004, and that the portion devoted to ethanol would rise to 20 percent in 2007. One of Vinod Khosla's fellow panelists in Aspen, Lester Brown, president of the Earth Policy Institute, fretted that there wouldn't be enough kernels left over for livestock. "In South Dakota, ethanol distilleries are already claiming over half that state's crop," he wrote. The Organisation for Economic Co-operation and Development concluded that if the United States were to produce enough corn-derived ethanol to juice 10 percent of its vehicles, it would take one-third of total farmland.

Greatly expanded ethanol use was problematic both in theory and in practice. Cars powered by ethanol don't get as good gas mileage as those running on imported petroleum. In 2005, an ethanol refinery in Iowa went into operation, powered by coal. And several others under construction intended to rely on the same cheap, polluting fuel, which is a little like eating a cheeseburger while riding a stationary bike. "If the biofuels industry is going to depend on coal, and these conversion plants release their CO_2 to the air, it could undo the global warming benefits of using ethanol," David Hawkins, climate director for the Natural Resources Defense Council in Washington, told the *Christian Science Monitor*.

As is the case with all early-stage commercial infrastructures—the telegraph, the railroad, the Internet—there were problems with connectivity. Ethanol lacked a national distribution system. The fuel was being produced in increasingly greater quantities, but at the end of 2006 only 6 million vehicles could run on ethanol. And while the government offered grants of $30,000 to gas stations to install E85 pumps, which could handle a blend of 85 percent ethanol and 15 percent petroleum, fewer than 1,000 stations had done so by the end of 2006. There were two in all of New York, fourteen in Texas, and one in Virginia. The ranks of skeptics also included millions of California citizens. In November, Proposition 87, the ballot initiative that would have taxed the Golden State's oil wells so that entrepreneurs like Vinod Khosla could turn golden waves of corn and wheat into commercial gold, failed to pass by a 55–45 majority.

The failure of Proposition 87 was only a small defeat in a much-larger war for state assistance to renewable energy. States, the great laboratories of democracies, have also been great incubators of bubbles. In the nineteenth century, many states provided vital assistance to early railroad and telegraph builders. In the twenty-first century, states are falling over themselves to assist the alternative energy industry. The Energy Department's Web site displays a smorgasbord of various state incentives for alternative fuels: a fuel tax reimbursement for taxis in Wisconsin that run on alternative fuels, a tax credit for buying hybrids in Colorado, and hundreds of other bonbons. Many states have decreed alternative energy industries by fiat by adapting renewable portfolio standards, which requires utilities to acquire a certain percentage or a certain volume of energy from renewable sources. By late 2006, twenty-three states had such standards. Among the most aggressive was California. In 2006, Governor Arnold Schwarzenegger signed a law declaring that California would derive 20 percent of its electricity from renewables by 2010. To reach this goal, the state would rely on two of its greatest natural resources: sunshine and technology entrepreneurs.

The solar industry, which started in the 1970s, grew slowly in the 1980s and 1990s. Shipments of photovoltaic cells rose from about 19,838 peak kilowatts in 2000 to nearly 135,000 in 2005. Production of solar-generated electricity rose from 493.4 million kilowatt-hours in 2000 to 579 million kilowatt-hours in 2005. But solar, at less than 1 percent of total U.S. electricity production, is set to receive a huge boost.

Virtually every state offers tax credits or financial incentives to home builders to include solar panels in new homes. The 2005 Energy Policy Act included grants to buyers of new homes with solar photovoltaic systems and a tax credit for 30 percent of the cost, up to $2,000. California, which was scarred deeply by its 2001 energy crisis, is taking the lead. As part of an effort to encourage the construction of 1 million solar roofs in the state, it has budgeted $3.2 billion in incentives to encourage home builders to include solar panels in new homes, and other efforts to encourage greater solar use.

As a result of such incentives, the industry is starting to gain scale. In June 2006, Nanosolar, Inc., based (where else?) in Palo Alto, raised $100 million from investors, among them Google founders Larry Page and Sergey Brin, to build the world's biggest solar cell factory. After striking a twenty-year energy supply deal with Southern California Edison, Stirling Energy Systems, based in Phoenix, began carpeting a four-square-mile portion of the Mojave Desert with solar dishes. "When completed, this power station will be the world's largest solar facility, capable of producing more electricity than all other U.S. solar projects combined," noted Stirling Energy. The company, which topped *Fast Company*'s Fast 50 list of hot companies, apparently isn't in it for the money. Its slogan reads: "Creating a brighter future for humanity through solar energy."

Just as ethanol inflated the price of corn, the emerging solar boom boosted the price of its key commodity, polysilicon. Prices of polysilicon soared from $30 per kilogram in 2003 to $73 in 2006, which was a problem for the semiconductor industry, a major consumer of the highly pure material. In 2006, Rhone Resch, president of the Solar Energy Industries Association, told the *Financial Times* that the solar energy industry would account for about half of polysilicon demand in 2006.

The growing demand wasn't bad for all semiconductor

companies. T. J. Rodgers, the famously libertarian founder of Cypress Semiconductor, is so dismissive of political correctness that he once told a shareholder activist, who happened to be a nun, to get lost. But he hasn't let his philosophy get in the way of minting millions on government subsidies. In November 2005, Cypress spun off to the public a unit that makes solar panels, SunPower, in a $139 million public offering. A year later, the company garnered a $2.6 billion market capitalization, dwarfing that of its former parent, and traded at 166 times earnings.

Solar energy may have been growing rapidly in the deserts of California and the Southwest, but its reliance on engineering and futuristic conducting materials made Silicon Valley its natural habitat. Throughout the San Francisco Bay Area, well-heeled engineers, many of whom got rich in the dot-com boom, were spending cash outfitting their homes with solar panels. In the fall of 2006, the most well-heeled engineers in the Valley—Google, Inc.—contracted with a company called Energy Innovations to install solar panels on the company's Mountain View headquarters. With this deal, a creature of the dot-com bust met a creature of the dot-com boom.

Energy Innovations is controlled by Bill Gross, the founder of Idealab, the incubator that spawned dot-com bubble-istas like eToys and PETsMART.com. But six years after the bust, Gross and Idealab were riding high again. The entrepreneur rummaged through his files and pulled out the unironic, revolutionary boosterism that was increasingly infiltrating the alternative energy industry. "Reinventing energy is a multitrillion-dollar opportunity. It's the next big disruption," Gross told *Wired* in July 2005. "It dwarfs any business opportunity in history." Uh-oh.

Indeed, by 2006, alternative energy started to look a lot like the Internet in 1997. Wall Street studs who had blackballed engineering dorks from their fraternities were once again lining up to kiss their feet. In an August 2006 *BusinessWeek* article titled, "Wall Street's New Love Affair," John Veech, a managing director at Lehman Brothers, described attending a renewable energy conference. "If you went five years ago you'd see a lot of ponytails," he told the authors, Emily Thornton and Adam Aston. "Now these conferences are packed with suits."

Once again, the guys at Kleiner, Perkins were at the forefront of a new revolution. Several KP partners, including John Doerr; Ray Lane, a former president at Oracle; and Bill Joy, the visionary former technology chief at Sun Microsystems, sat for a photo in a *Newsweek* section on clean energy investing. Wearing matching khaki pants and blue oxford shirts (no tie, one button open), they looked like superannuated Gap salesmen. They had decided to plunge $200 million of their $600 million fund into what was now being called cleantech. "Now we are dealing not with a sector of billions, but we're dealing with a sector of trillions," Lane told the *Wall Street Journal* in the fall of 2006. "This is bigger than the Internet, I think by an order of magnitude. Maybe two. I'm talking the entire energy industry."

It wasn't just ethanol and solar. Wind energy production capacity rose from 2,490 megawatts in 1999 to 9,149 in 2005. And the professional investors weren't alone. In March 2005, the PowerShares WilderHill Clean Energy Portfolio exchange traded fund, composed of forty publicly traded stocks in the alternative energy and energy space, began trading. The personal finance–industrial complex began to focus on alternative energy stocks. "Articles in business magazines detailing ways readers can profit from soaring energy prices are well on the way to replacing ones about how to make money in real estate," Paul Brown noted in the *New York Times* in July 2006.

In 2005 and 2006, alternative energy was crossing over from the investment world into far larger realms: popular culture and consumer culture. There was no lame sitcom about a hot young professional moving back home to the small farm town in Iowa where she grew up to start an ethanol plant. But Al Gore's *An Inconvenient Truth,* the 102nd-largest-grossing movie of 2006, won an Academy Award. The *Vanity Fair* green issue, in April 2006, featured such prominent environmentalists as Julia Roberts and George Clooney. *Wired* and *Business 2.0,* the surviving print bibles of the dot-com boom, were filled with stories about light-emitting diodes, zero-emission cars, rechargeable fuel cells, and hackers who pimp their Prius hybrids to run even farther on electricity.

Many of the same companies that went business casual and funded Internet start-ups in the 1990s are now going green. As part of an effort to stamp his own imprint on the company, General Electric CEO Jeff Immelt, who took over from icon Jack Welch in 2001, launched an ecomagination initiative. By 2010, GE plans to ring up $20 billion in annual sales of eco-friendly products—wind turbines, fuel-efficient engines, energy-sipping appliances, solar energy panels, and water treatment systems.

GE also tried to tap into the greatest power source known to modern man: American consumers. It hooked up with Wal-Mart to push the sale of low-emitting, long-lasting compact fluorescent bulbs. In fact, in 2006, it often seemed as if the real Wal-Mart had been kidnapped and replaced by a refugee from a 1960s-era commune. The company set up in-store displays for the DVD of *An Inconvenient Truth*, paired with coupons and mail-in rebates for compact fluorescent bulbs. It built experimental green stores equipped with solar panels and embarked on a serious effort to double the fuel efficiency of its monster trucking fleet by 2015. In an interview in the spring of 2006, Wal-Mart CEO Lee Scott sounded more like the head of the Sierra Club than a member of the Business Roundtable: "I had embraced this idea that the world's climate is changing and that man played a part in that, and that Wal-Mart can play a part in reducing man's impact."

The greening of Wal-Mart roughly coincided with the retailer's effort, thus far unsuccessful, to appeal to higher-income shoppers. As in prior Pop! episodes, a portion of the dollars invested in the exciting new area are being deployed to build mental infrastructure. And in this context, that meant fostering a greater consumer awareness of energy and energy-related products, especially among higher-end consumers. For pretty much the entire stretch of human history, energy—fire, coal, whale oil, petroleum—has been a commodity. These days, however, energy is rapidly becoming a branded consumer product. And for many, it has become a status symbol. With the advent of the Prius and Lexus hybrids, conspicuous consumption of vehicles testifies to the owners' parsimonious consumption of gasoline. (The generous federal tax credit of up to $3,150 helps defray the high cost of hybrids.)

In the era of deregulated utilities, energy is something that is no longer simply provided—it is branded, marketed, and sold. In posh suburbs, neighbors impress one another by dropping the names of Caribbean resorts they've visited. Increasingly, however, they do so by pointing out that they purchase wind energy from the local utility, or that the pool is heated in part by a solar cover. Amid the raging housing boom, some landlords tried to differentiate their increasingly branded products by affixing green labels on condominium projects. The Solaire, a rental building that opened in New York City's Tribeca in 2003, was fitted out with photovoltaic cells, rainwater storage equipment for the roof garden, and a bike storage room.

Kermit the Frog, who proclaimed, "It's not easy being green," had it all wrong. More and more companies are finding it easier to be green. Companies like Vail Resorts and Whole Foods have made their use of alternative energy or their efforts to become carbon neutral a part of the overall marketing message. Richard Branson pledged to funnel profits from his air and rail transport businesses into a new alternative fuel subisidary, which *Business 2.0* featured as one of "The Best Business Ideas in the World." Waste Management, the garbage collection company, urges the public to "Think Green. Think Waste Management." (The company produces methane from the vast piles of stinking refuse it collects.) Tyson Foods, the gigantic chicken processor, has been suffering due to the ethanol-inspired rise in the price of corn, so it's joining the crowd. In 2006, Tyson created a subsidiary, Tyson Renewable Energy, to "commercialize the company's vast supply of animal fat into biofuels."

Slowly but surely, the last of the skeptics are being converted. Rupert Murdoch, the CEO least likely to exhibit politically correct behavior, finally joined the crowd. "I have to admit that, until recently, I was somewhat wary of the warming debate. I believe it is now our responsibility to take the lead on this issue," Murdoch piously told a conference in Tokyo in November 2006. "The earth deserves the benefit of the doubt." Even the most stubborn, reality-denying, argument-impervious chief executive in America bought in to the promise of alternative energy. In his 2006 State of the Union address, President Bush waxed rhapsodic about the wonder-working power of switchgrass. "We'll also fund additional research in cutting-edge methods of producing ethanol, not just from corn, but from wood chips and stalks, or switchgrass," he said. "Our goal is to make this new kind of ethanol practical and competitive within six years."

So by the end of 2006, all the ingredients for a bubble seemed to be in place: the money and the absurdly optimistic projections, the huge investments in physical and mental infrastructure, the hype and the inflated commodities, the crossover into popular culture. As with prior booms, the alternative energy boom has created jobs, stimulated a burst of innovation and capital formation, and created new businesses. The United States is seeing growth not just in ethanol refiners, but in companies that install solar panels and refit gas stations to handle ethanol.

But it's not quite there yet. Ethanol stocks have already cooled. And it's possible that with so much attention being paid to the real estate bubble, Americans have become somewhat more circumspect about bidding up another class of assets so rapidly. As 2007 dawned, alternative energy was half a bubble—let's call it a bub.

What's more, unlike the previous episodes, the Pop! dynamic is not exclusively an American phenomenon. Asia has seen huge growth in the palm oil business. The largest solar panel company in the world is Suntech, a Chinese firm. Renewable Energy Corp., which makes solar components, closed its first day of trading in 2006 with a remarkable $7.7 billion market value; the IPO was on the company's home exchange, in Oslo, Norway. Germany has far more generous solar subsidies than the United States, and Brazil, which rivals the United States in ethanol production, has a far more developed distribution infrastructure. In Japan, consumers and businesses buy solar panel systems in the absence of government incentives. This may be the first investment boom of the Flat World era. As a result, the United States may not reap the same type of competitive advantage from overinvesting in a new commercial infrastructure as it has in the past.

As in previous episodes, many investments don't seem to make sense without government subsidies. If the past is any guide, many of the companies funded in recent years will lose money. And as they do so, they will start rate wars. Those who entered too late, or paid too much for acquisitions at the wrong time, or relied too much on debt will find themselves in trouble when excess capacity develops, or if the price of oil falls, or if the government ends certain sub-sidies, or if distribution bottlenecks materialize. If we are in the midst of a bubble, it will surely result in plenty of bankruptcies, and it will surely leave behind a great deal of infrastructure that others can use: ethanol stations, wind farms, and solar-panel makers. As the *Economist* put it: "The flood of money into clean energy is better news for society than it is for investors."

Of course, the statement could have been made about the telegraph in the 1850s, the railroad in the early 1890s, and the dot-com/fiber-optic complex in the 1990s. But in its hardheaded way, the *Economist* was pointing out that in a free market where competition is based almost solely on price, very few of these alternative energy businesses seem to have sound models, given current market dynamics. True enough. But as history teaches, that's a rather short-sighted view. When it comes to truly revolutionary tech-nologies, you have to look beyond the impending crash. All it takes is a little bit of eco-imagination.

Skeptics accurately note that with its high installa-tion costs, solar energy doesn't light up homes more cheaply than coal-fired plants. But make a few adjustments in the Excel spreadsheet. Ratchet up the price of non-solar-produced energy 15 percent (for impending carbon taxes), ratchet down the price of a solar installation by 50 percent, and then factor in improved efficiency of solar panels. In

ten years, solar could be a brilliant economic *and* environ-
mental idea. Consider how engineers have managed to
bring down the price of computers or big-screen televisions
or the price of wind-generated energy. Thanks to improved
turbines, the cost of producing wind power has fallen from
between $0.08 and $0.10 per kilowatt-hour in 1990 to between $0.035 and $0.04 per kilowatt-hour today. And the
Six Sigma black belts and ninjas at GE's wind turbine unit
aren't done yet.

A hybrid Toyota Camry costs about $3,000 more than a
gas-only Camry, and yet a hybrid driver probably saves only
about $500 per year in gas. But what if gas is $3.50 or $4.00
a gallon (think what will happen when the Chinese and In-
dians really start to drive)? And what if that hybrid can be
plugged in to juice the battery further, eliminating the need
for more gas purchase? And what if that electric power
comes from solar power or wind? And what if the volume
of Toyota's production of hybrids rises from about 200,000
today to, say, 800,000? The hybrid will make much more
economic sense.

Without falling into the sort of optimism that leads to
melt-ups, it is not too hard to imagine that the vast sums being plowed into developing alternative energy resources,
products, and services will lead to incremental improve-
ments and perhaps to some revolutionary breakthroughs.
And as more giant companies such as Wal-Mart become

consumers and vendors of alternative-energy products and services, the industry will gain scale—a development that leads to price reductions for all consumers.

Back in 1975, a person who projected that (a) the United States would need half as much energy to produce a dollar of gross domestic product in 2005 as it did in 1975, and (b) the economy would grow by a factor of 7.6 in those years of uninterrupted declines in energy intensity, would have been dismissed as a Pollyanna. And yet, three decades later, here we are. The prospects look pretty good for further declines in energy intensity and for further declines in the impact on the environment—the geopolitical environment and the atmospheric environment—exacted by our use of energy. A real bubble would surely help this process along.

We need more: a CNBC special and a half-dozen best-selling books on how each person can be his or her own power producer. Four reality shows in which families compete to build solar panels, harvest corn, and erect wind turbines. We need George Gilder to promote a start-up that transmits ethanol via solar-powered fiber-optic cables. We need a dozen alternative energy ETFs and a $1 billion windpower IPO. We need Gary Winnick to find his way out of his massive home and put the junk bond band back together to fund a global solar panel behemoth. We need the government to double down, to go long and go deep on its commitment to renewables. We need more cockeyed legislation urging utilities to get 30 percent of electricity from renewables by 2010, and more studies, like the one the Rand Institute issued in 2006, suggesting that renewable energy could supply up to one-quarter of the U.S. energy supply in 2025. We need the Big Three automakers, who pledge to make 50 percent of their new cars compatible with alternative fuel by 2012, to up that pledge to 100 percent, and by 2009.

No, we're not quite there yet. But, God willing, it could happen.

CONCLUSION

Bubbles are hot. In recent years, analysts have hastened to stamp the scarlet *B* on a host of phenomena. In 2003, George Soros issued a warning with *The Bubble in American Supremacy*. In August 2005, noting with alarm the trend of $319 True Religion jeans, Michelle Leder warned in *Slate* of an impending denim bubble. In 2006, the media identified speculative mania in oil and credit derivatives and private equity and leveraged buyouts. On Amazon .com, bubble-ologists can browse such volumes as *Bubble After Bubble in the Ongoing Bubble Boom*, or *America's Bubble Economy: Profit When It Pops*, or *Bubbles, Booms, and Busts*. At times, it seems as if the United States is simply a 3.54-million-square-mile incubator.

Our recently concluded breakneck tour through the past sesquicentury teaches us that bubbles that leave behind a usable commercial infrastructure are net positives. And yet it is important not to be too sanguine about outbursts of investor enthusiasm. For all the good times they span on the way up, and in the long term, bubbles cause a great deal of short-term pain, loss, and embarrassment.

And some bubbles leave us with bubkes. Given the role of government and policy-makers in fomenting and sustaining bubbles, it is therefore natural to wonder, should the Federal Reserve, the White House, or Congress try to stop bubbles from developing? When asset prices are deemed dangerously high, should the Federal Reserve raise interest rates to choke off speculation? Should Congress phase out tax credits for an exciting new technology when private sector capital floods into the sector?

Clearly, the answer to all three questions is a resounding no. Bubbles are too much fun, and nobody wants to be a buzz kill. More practically, it is difficult to see how entities as fallible and error prone as state and federal governments could manage bubbles successfully. It's easy to read back through history and conclude what Congress or the president or the Federal Reserve should have done or should not have done at a particular moment. But history unfolds in real time and in a contingent manner. At any given moment, when policy-makers are confronted with a choice— to back a second telegraph line, or to give land grants to a railroad, or to scale back a tax credit for hybrid vehicles— they have no clue how events will unfold.

Bubbles *have* produced observable patterns. But there is nothing predetermined about the way in which investment enthusiasms lead to infrastructure bubbles, or the timing of the pop, or the way in which the system processes the collapse. As a species, our record of forecasting short-term macroeconomic developments is rather poor. And our record of forecasting long-term macroeconomic developments is even worse. The long-term benefits that result from bubbles are never apparent when they are raging. In 1998, investors believed everybody would get rich by investing in Amazon.com and WorldCom, not in Google.

Expecting the government to manage and control the way in which new technologies and business concepts are rolled out would also require a fundamental reimagination of the relationship between the public and private sectors. To be sure, the United States has always been in the business of subsidizing and favoring certain industries. But to a large degree, it does so in spite of itself. The support doesn't arise organically, but rather as a result of lobbying. Samuel Morse begged a reluctant Congress to fund the first telegraph line. Lobbyists, the creation of railroad companies, pressured the government to finance the transcontinental railroads, and to provide incentives for investments in the Internet, housing, and alternative energy.

Despite Alexander Hamilton's energetic urgings, the U.S. government has generally shunned the role of central planner for nearly 220 years. Which is all to the good. Markets may not be perfectly efficient (how else to account for the existence of the Olive Garden?). But they're more efficient than the alternative. And so rather than focus on how they can prevent bubbles, policy-makers should focus on how to ensure that the nation's systems continue to allow the economy to recover from bubbles after they burst.

Besides, if some omniscient Bureau of Bubble Management were to be tasked with the capacity to halt enthusiasms before they got out of control, we wouldn't necessarily want it to do so. "I hold it, that a little rebellion, now and then, is a good thing, and as necessary in the political world as storms in the physical," Thomas Jefferson wrote to James Madison in 1787. In the economic realm, a little rebellion, now and then, is a good thing, too. And bubbles, entrepreneurial storms that disrupt the existing commercial order, provide shots of adrenaline. The enthusiasm they generate has led successive generations of entrepreneurs to open new territory for settlement, to create valuable new infrastructure, to spur innovation, and to push people to work, invest, and spend at a higher level—all in pursuit of promised massive short-term gains.

If every new technology were rolled out rationally (as has generally been the case in Europe), if Americans collectively adopted the attitude that the economy and each of its constituent sectors would grow at a staid 2 percent annual pace, year in and year out, people wouldn't rush headlong to start new enterprises. The excess capacity that proves such a spur to mass adoption, scale, innovation, and growth would not develop. The United States would be a less frenetic place, yes, but also a less happy, optimistic, and useful one.

In fact, the case can be made that we need the Pop! mentality now more than ever. In his impressive book *The Moral Consequences of Economic Growth*, Harvard economist Benjamin Friedman shrewdly makes the liberal case for higher growth. Friedman argues that much of what is good and great about modernity—tolerance and democracy, rights and social mobility—is made possible by expanding economies. So while bubbles certainly stimulate a large amount of unethical and immoral behavior, the sort of rapid growth they can help spur is deeply moral. In the United States today, rapid growth has the capacity to paper over conflicts and cleanse sins. An economy that grows at 3 percent instead of 1 percent can more easily accommodate immigrants and new entrants to the workforce, allow people to move into the middle class, and improve shaky personal and government finances. In part due to outbursts of investor enthusiasm, Americans have largely been spared the confidence-killing ennui of slow growth that has hobbled Europe and Japan.

Given the long-term benefits they can produce and their potential to help forge new industries, bubbles shouldn't be feared so much as regarded with concern and respected. Just so, we shouldn't be so hard on ourselves when we get caught up in them and act stupidly. Nor should we be so hard on the promoters who snookered us into believing.

In fact, historically speaking, we owe a debt of gratitude to methodless enthusiasts like Henry O'Reilly and Cyrus Field, to mindless empire builders like Jay Gould, to pie-in-the-sky optimists like John J. Raskob and Charles Mitchell, to failed prophets like George Gilder and Gary Winnick, to headstrong bulls like David Lereah and Robert Toll, and to assured technophiles like Bill Gross and Vinod Khosla—and to all the Henry Hills and Lyle Lanleys who have worked so hard over the years to convince us to plunge our hard-earned money into new business ideas. They didn't tell us anything we didn't want to hear or believe.

Taking the long view, the exploits and shenanigans of bubble-era promoters look less self-interested and more selfless. We should all try to take a similarly long view about our own bubble-era behavior. In those low, postbust moments of self-loathing and recrimination, those of us cursed with ever-shorter attention spans—which is to say, all of us—must will ourselves to take the long view. Those who do so will see their self-esteem rise. As important, they will find that a long view can help them profit from their knowledge of the Pop! dynamic.

Unless you're the chief executive officer of one of the many companies whose boards of directors were nice enough to backdate options, it's impossible to invest money with hindsight. Nonetheless, looking back, clear themes emerge as to how investors should play these cycles. Nobody declares when a bubble has started or ended. But even

amateurs should be able to detect the telltale s'
frastructure bubble: the extrapolation of sho:
ad infinitum, the emergence of high-profile promoters, ...
crossover into popular culture, the ritual bludgeoning of
the skeptics, the development of excess capacity. The signs
of the pop are easily detectable as well: the sickening drop
in asset prices, the widespread denial and fruitless bottom-
calling, the rage, grief, and ultimate acceptance.

If you think a bubble is developing, or has just ended,
these six rules might help you profit—or at least help you
avoid the type of losses your blowhard brother-in-law will
suffer.

1. *Get long the commodities.* Prices of commodities and raw
materials are generally leading indicators. In virtually every Pop! cycle, infrastructure build-out has stimulated
sharply higher demand for crucial raw materials and commodities. The telegraph was a boon to copper miners and
manufacturers of copper wire. The burst in railroad construction helped the steel industry gain critical mass. The
prices of wood, cement, and gypsum took flight during the
real estate boom, just as corn and polysilicon became great
investments when alternative energy heated up.

Amid booms, those who produce raw materials gain
pricing power early in the cycle, and maintain it even as excess capacity arises. Since they have shorter product cycles—
commodities are generally grown, mined, or harvested to be

used immediately—their margins don't suffer as badly when the market turns. Value-adding manufacturers buy raw materials and string up wires, lay rails, and build homes and ethanol plants based on an anticipated flow of business over several years. So when excess capacity triggers price wars, they, not the commodity producers, are left holding the bag.

2. *Avoid the consolidators during the upswing.* As bubble-era optimism takes hold, entrepreneurs and companies show a willingness to double down, to increase their exposure to the hot sector, and to pay any price to guarantee a slice of the endlessly profitable market. But just as there is too much money chasing the same business, there is too much money chasing the same assets. With money easy to come by, empire builders are eager to spend. Companies who use cash or stock to expand when bubbles are in full swing inevitably leverage up and pay too much, rendering themselves ill-equipped to handle a downturn. As Jimmy Cliff put it, "the harder they come, the harder they fall."

Most of the telegraph companies that sought greater scale in the 1840s failed quickly. Railroads that bulked up, merged, and acquired systems in the late 1880s simply sank faster when price wars exacted their toll. Perhaps the most foolhardy acquisitions of all time were seen in the dot-com/fiber-optic era. Yahoo! paid $5.7 billion in its stock for Broadcast.com in 1999. The high-speed Internet company

@Home acquired Excite for $7.2 billion in stock in May 1999; twenty-nine months later, the merged company went bust. WorldCom took on unsustainable loads of debt to buy MCI and UUNET at exactly the wrong time. In 2006, Wachovia paid $25.5 billion for California mortgage lender Golden West Financial. And in 2006, Wall Street firms bought subprime mortgage lenders just as things were about to sour. These latter acquisitions will likely act as drags on earnings for years.

3. *Balance sheets matter.* Bubbles inspire tidal waves of hype, projections, and dream spinning. But amid all the excitement over new technologies and economic concepts, a mundane, boring factor determines who shall live and who shall die: the balance sheet. And while the advantages provided by innovative technology and business plans don't last particularly long, fiscal sanity amid investment insanity can pay long-term dividends. When bubbles turn to busts, debt kills.

Investors should carefully examine two types of debt. The first is the use of debt to construct or expand businesses. The poorly capitalized telegraph and railroad firms in the nineteenth century, and the seemingly overcapitalized fiber-optic network firms in the late twentieth century, never had a prayer because absurdly optimistic projections about pricing and traffic failed to materialize. High debt levels left them no margin for error.

A second form of debt can be just as lethal: vendor financing. In bubbles, businesses frequently double down by lending to customers. During the frenzy, such practices supercharge earnings. But when cold winds begin to blow, vendor financers catch double pneumonia. In the 1920s, banks like National City, which sold securities, also lent vast sums of cash to customers so that they could buy securities. When the crash came, the bank was doubly crushed: the demand for securities failed, and it got stuck with bad debt. In the 1990s, companies like Nortel and Lucent, which sold fiber-optic network equipment, lent billions of dollars to fiber-optic network builders. When the crash came, they were doubly crushed. Demand for their products plummeted, and they found themselves with billions of dollars of uncollectible debt on their balance sheets. Home builders who took advantage of cheap money to build sideline businesses in mortgages or in lending money to home purchasers, will face a similar double whammy.

4. *Be a consolidator (or invest in one) after the fall.* Bubbles are bipolar. The frenzy and irrational optimism that break out during the upswing swiftly morph into paralysis and irrational pessimism come the bust. So when erstwhile promoters flee the country and hire defense lawyers, when journalists are holed up in libraries writing quickie scandal accounts, when me-too businesses that entered the industry at the top look to get out—that's the time to buy.

In many instances, the failed bubble-era companies were undone by poor capital structures and business models fueled by unrealistic assumptions. Bankruptcy proceedings and time fix both those problems. In the cases of the telegraph, the railroad, and the fiber-optic/dot-com bubbles, demand for the services continued to rise postbust. And when new operators were able to assume control after shedding or decreasing debt, they found themselves in control of viable businesses. They reduced fixed costs, slashed operating expenses, and were thus the first to benefit when the projected demand finally started to materialize. In the 1890s, J. P. Morgan, Jacob Schiff, and Edward Harriman picked through the railroad wreckage to assemble large, integrated systems on the cheap. Charles Merrill positioned himself nicely for a long-term revival by consolidating the brokerage business in the late 1930s. This decade, Level 3 and Global Crossing, which acquired new management and ownership after its bankruptcy, have successfully acquired distressed assets. If the ethanol business turns into popcorn, my money would be on ADM, whose conservative balance sheet and diversified business should allow it to survive and consolidate.

5. *Be a bandwidth hog (or invest in one)*. During infrastructure bubbles, bandwidth hogs—companies whose business models rest on distributing and transmitting products and services through a commercial infrastructure—are easily

frustrated. Telegraph systems that refused to interconnect, railroads running on different gauges, and the slow rollout of residential broadband were poison to the companies who relied on the services that failed to work as advertised. But in the long term, bandwidth hogs are among the biggest beneficiaries of excess capacity. The costs they pay to ship goods and services plummet even as the promotional efforts of infrastructure builders rope in legions of new users.

Once telegraph became a cheap, pervasive utility, power users like news services and stock brokerages became successful businesses. Railroad bandwidth hogs—everyone from Sears and Montgomery Ward to shippers of cattle, produce, and packaged goods—thrived once railroads became reliable, seamless networks. In this decade, a host of businesses that rely on universal, cheap broadband have attracted investment and minted money for their founders, among them Google, YouTube, MySpace, and Skype.

6. *Serve the new users.* Businesses that provide services to bandwidth hogs—and to the customers of bandwidth hogs—seem small during the bubble, and even smaller during the bust. But they can be big postbust winners. Identifying or building such companies, however, requires a great deal of imagination in addition to perseverance. One of the salient characteristics of the Pop! dynamic is the way in

which new infrastructure creates business opportunities that were not evident or imagined during the bubble. As Carlota Perez reminds us: "Railways were first developed to help get coal out of the mines; their real significance as the main means of transporting people and goods was difficult to even imagine in a world of canals, turnpikes and horses." Just so, the Internet, first seen as a more efficient postal system, has become a means of distributing a stunning range of products: software, entertainment, gift cards, stocks, medical imagery, and telephony.

The railroad didn't just prove to be a boon to mail-order retailers and food processors, it provided opportunities for travel agents and shipping companies. The New Deal economic infrastructure, which helped convince Americans it was safe to bank and invest, helped banks and brokerage firms. But it also paved the way for industries that serviced new borrowers and investors, such as credit card companies and asset managers. In this decade, companies that enable people to set up shop on the Web, or that help businesses conduct transactions online—from VeriSign to the blogging software company Six Apart—have prospered by servicing new users who continued to flood into the medium. And while many of the alternative energy infrastructure firms may fail, businesses that maintain and upgrade residential solar installations, or that provide kits that allow existing automobiles to run on ethanol, may succeed.

Of course, it goes without saying that the past is no guide to future performance. And that bromide doesn't apply only to individuals who hope to profit from the Pop! cycle. It applies as well to economies and countries. Given the American experience, one might logically conclude that it would be a smart move for governments in slow-growing developed economies, or in developing countries that need bursts of investment to catch up, to mimic the United States and kick-start bubbles. But like the corporate media efforts to create viral media campaigns, intentional efforts to generate excess investment would be bound to fail. Bubbles bubble up, not down.

And I believe the process surrounding bubbles will remain an important component of American exceptionalism. To an astonishing degree, the United States has imposed its commercial culture, consumer culture, popular culture, and financial culture on the rest of the world. It stands to reason that just as other countries adopt Starbucks and Google, private equity and Brangelina, they may also adopt the American habit of making the best out of bubbles. After all, it is comparatively easy for a central government to enact policies that encourage overbuilding. Just look at China, a veritable kingdom of excess capacity.

But excess physical infrastructure is only half the story. Ultimately, it is the mental infrastructure built in bubbles— and the mental infrastructure that supports the American economic system—that helps turn lemons into lemonade.

And while it is comparatively easy to mimic American business tactics, foreigners will have a tough time mimicking the American mindset.

In a flat world, more than ever, a national economy is much more than the sum of its hard assets—factories, stores, railroads, natural resources. Increasingly, the difference between champions and chumps resides in so-called intangible assets: brands, research and development, patents, and a highly functional legal and regulatory system. Such assets are frequently difficult to value, yet they can be monetized and borrowed against. And they can provide a significant competitive advantage. I would argue that a nation's history and reputation also constitute valuable intangible assets.

In a February 2006 *BusinessWeek* cover story, economics correspondent Michael Mandel argued that such intangible assets, or "dark matter," bolster the nation's competitive position and function as a hidden source of strength. The proven ability of this country to nurture talent, to commercialize innovation, and to protect property and profits allows the government to borrow at low costs, and allows Americans to sell their stock, real estate, and corporate assets to foreigners high multiples. In an era when investors can choose from literally hundreds of markets in which to invest, foreigners continue to flock to the United States and to U.S. assets.

But dark matter also resides in Americans' collective

gray matter. And it could be that our ultimate intangible asset is the collective mindset—the mental infrastructure—that has driven the episodes of this book. The tendency to methodless enthusiasm, the habit of periodically succumbing to irrational exuberance and excessive optimism, the ability to pivot quickly to practicality, the sangfroid to write off debts and losses, and the pluck to heed the advice Jerome Kern dispensed in the middle of the Depression.

> *Don't lose your confidence if you slip*
> *Be grateful for a pleasant trip,*
> *And pick yourself up, dust yourself off,*
> *Start all over again.*

When it comes to business, the United States is like a shooting guard, who, heedless of the airball he hoisted a minute before, stands twenty-three feet from the basket and demands the ball as the clock ticks down. Excess confidence? A lack of awareness of one's limitations? Sure. But it also signifies an ability to not let recent failure stymie new efforts.

More so than any other country on earth, the United States celebrates and glorifies winners, and marginalizes and despises losers. But as tens of millions of immigrants have learned over the years, this is also the nation of the second chance. And in the United States, failure and bankruptcy do not signify an end to the capitalist process. Chapter 11 isn't a final resting place for businesses or ideas or trends. "It's a place where things are dealt with in an orderly fashion," as Stephen Cooper, the head of the busy turnaround firm Kroll Zolfo Cooper puts it.

The attitudes and emotions that enable America to make so much out of new technologies, new ideas, and new ways of doing business are deeply embedded in the national character. It's a complex combination of idealism and greed, of brilliant individual innovation and mindless crowd-following, of a tolerance for chaos and a penchant for order, of a powerful desire to change the world coexisting with an equally powerful desire to create vast private fortunes. Americans have always believed that regardless of the grim reality we face, regardless of the stupid decisions and venal behavior that got us into the present mess, that tomorrow will be better. It's there in the rhetoric of Franklin Delano Roosevelt, in the lyrics of Jerome Kern, and in the self-affirmation of Heather Whitestone, the deaf girl from Alabama who became Miss America in 1995: "The last four letters of American are 'I Can.' "

It is there, too, in the quintessential work of American self-invention, self-destruction, and moving on. F. Scott Fitzgerald's *The Great Gatsby* is an elegant and elegiac tale about money and dreamers, the lure of cash and the tragedy of disappointment, the rise and fall of a self-made tale spinner, and the desire to be deceived. It is easy to paint Jay Gatsby, né James Gatz, who faked his Oxford education and supported a philoaristocratic lifestyle through bootlegging, as the ultimate cynic. But in the end, that's not what his friend and neighbor thought. "Gatsby believed in the green light, the orgiastic future that year by year recedes before us," Nick Carraway concluded. "It eluded us then, but that's no matter—tomorrow we will run faster, stretch out our arms farther. . . . And one fine morning—"

ACKNOWLEDGMENTS

I owe an enormous debt of gratitude to the historians and journalists who have covered, chronicled, and interpreted the episodes described in this book. In the text, the note on sources, and in the endnotes, which will appear on my Web site—www.danielgross.net—I have tried to fully credit the many sources on which I relied. Beyond attribution, I'd like to offer a collective thank-you to the brave souls who have stood in the eyes of bubbles and have tried to make sense of their bloody aftermath. Without the work of giants like John Kenneth Galbraith and John Brooks, this dwarf would have no shoulders on which to stand.

Many other people deserve a share of the credit for helping bring this book to fruition. I first started thinking about the ways in which excess capacity can spur long-term growth and innovation in 2001, while I was a fellow at the New America Foundation. Gordon Silverstein, Sherle Schwenninger, and Ted Halstead afforded me the time and freedom to think beyond immediate deadlines, and encouraged me to pursue the connection between developments in the private sector and public policy.

ACKNOWLEDGMENTS

The kernels of this book lie in an op-ed that appeared in 2001 in the *New York Times*, which was commissioned by Mary Suh, and in an essay that appeared in the March 2002 *Milken Institute Review*, which was edited by Peter Passell.

I believe in recycling. Accordingly, bits and pieces of this book have appeared in articles spread among several publications in the past two years. My thanks to Hugo Lindgren at *New York*, Mark Robinson at *Wired*, and Jeff Sommer and Katy Roberts at the *New York Times* for their patronage, indulgence, and editing skills.

Slate, my part-time home for nearly five years, has contributed to this project in many ways. The reporting for several "Moneybox" columns helped fuel the last three chapters of the book. Editor Jacob Weisberg suggested the title. Aside from editing my column brilliantly, deputy editor David Plotz read the whole manuscript, provided valuable comments, and was understanding when I needed to scale back my writing to carve out time to finish the book. Every week, *Slate*'s stellar copy-editing crew saves me from mistakes and makes me look far more thorough and articulate than I am.

Over the past two years, several friends, colleagues, sources, and relatives have assisted in one or more of the following ways: by providing data and sources, by offering feedback, or just by nodding and stifling yawns as I held forth on the glories of bubbles. My thanks to: Jesse Eisinger, Leon Gross, Zachary Karabell, Adam Lashinsky, Barry

Ritholtz, Gavriel Rosenfeld, and Mark Zandi. Jonathan Rosenberg, who read a large chunk of the manuscript and provided sage comments, deserves special mention.

This project brought me back in touch with the New America Foundation, where Simone Frank provided valuable administrative support.

Several committed professionals helped conjure this book into being. My agent, Sloan Harris, is a forceful advocate whose ability to navigate the literary marketplace is matched by his ability to tolerate client neuroses. My thanks to him and the staff at International Creative Management. Marion Maneker is the rare publisher who gets it, and who knows deftly how to wield the carrot (lunch at Aquavit) and the stick (good-natured but persistent nudging about deadlines). Marion and his team at Collins transformed this book from a mass of words into a finished product with remarkable speed. Sarah Brown shepherded the manuscript through production, Anne Greenberg and Traci Maynigo copy-edited the book, Jaime Putorti crafted an engaging design, editorial production was supervised by Marina Padakis, print production by Nyamekye Waliyaya, publicity by Beth Mellow, and marketing by Angie Lee.

Without the unconditional love and support of my wife, Candice Savin, I couldn't get through the week—let alone finish a book. For twelve years, she has been my best friend, teammate, and constant reality-check. Candi read every single word of this book, and offered many suggestions to improve it. And she endured with good cheer the annoyance of having a deadline-addled writer moping around the house.

This book is dedicated to our children, Aliza and Ethan, whose spirits light up our world. They are one of the main reasons I am exhausted at night. And they are the main reason I can't wait to get up in the morning. They are our lives and lengthen our days.

D.G.
Westport, Ct.
January 2007

SOURCES

CHAPTER ONE

The essential literature on bubbles and investment mania includes: Charles Mackay, *Extraordinary Popular Delusions and the Madness of Crowds* (Wiley, 1996); Charles Kindleberger, *Manias, Panics, and Crashes* (Basic Books, 1978); John Kenneth Galbraith, *The Great Crash, 1929* (Houghton Mifflin, 1997); Robert Shiller, *Irrational Exuberance* (Princeton University Press, 2000); Roger Lowenstein, *Origins of the Crash: The Great Bubble and Its Undoing* (Penguin, 2004); Edward Chancellor, *Devil Take the Hindmost: A History of Financial Speculation* (MacMillan, 1999); Carlota Perez, *Technological Revolutions and Financial Capital: The Dynamics of Bubbles and Golden Ages* (Edward Elgar, 2002).

Books on the broad sweep of American history that have informed this book include Louis Hartz, *The Liberal Tradition in America* (Harcourt Brace Jovanovich, 1991); John Gartner, *The Hypomanic Edge* (Simon & Schuster,

2005); Deborah Spar, *Ruling the Waves: Cycles of Discovery, Chaos, and Wealth from the Compass to the Internet* (Harcourt, 2001); and Zachary Karabell, *A Visionary Nation: Four Centuries of American Dreams and What Lies Ahead* (HarperCollins, 2001). For good overviews of American business history, see Harold Evans, *They Made America* (Little Brown, 2004); and the works of Alfred D. Chandler, Jr., especially *Scale and Scope: the Dynamics of Industrial Capitalism* (Belknap, 1990); and *The Visible Hand: The Managerial Revolution in American Business* (Belknap, 1977); Joseph Schumpeter laid out his theory of creative destruction in *Capitalism, Socialism and Democracy* (1942).

David Denby, *American Sucker* (Little, Brown, 2004), is an excellent example of post-bust self-flagellation, while Michael Dertouzos, *What Will Be: How the New World of Information Will Change Our Lives* (HarperEdge, 1997); James Glassman and Kevin Hassett, *Dow 36,000* (Times Business, 1999); David Lereah, *Are You Missing the Real Estate Boom?: The Boom Will Not Bust and Why Property Values Will Continue to Climb Through the End of the Decade—And How to Profit from Them* (Currency, 2005), are fine examples of the optimistic mindset that takes hold during bubbles.

CHAPTER TWO

The earliest histories of the telegraph include Charles Briggs and August Maverick, *The Story of the Telegraph and a History of the Great Atlantic Cable* (Rudd & Carleton, 1858), and Henry Field, *History of the Atlantic Telegraph* (Scribner, 1893). The best single source on the early history of the telegraph is Robert Luther Thompson, *Wiring a Continent: The History of the Telegraph Industry in the United States, 1832–1866* (Princeton University Press, 1947). The best modern works on telegraphic history include Tom Standage, *The Victorian Internet* (Weidenfeld & Nicolson, 1998); John Steele Gordon, *Thread Across the Ocean: The Heroic Story of the Transatlantic Cable* (New York: Walker & Co., 2002). Debora Spar, *Ruling the Waves*, has a good chapter on the telegraph.

Other sources on the development of the telegraph include: Richard B. Du Boff, "Business Demand and the Development of the Telegraph in the United States, 1844–1860," *The Business History Review*, Vol. 54, No. 4 (Winter, 1980); Frederick Williams; *The Communications Revolution* (Sage Publications, 1982), Ken Beauchamp, *History of Telegraphy* (London: Institution of Electrical Engineers, 2001); Lewis Coe, *The Telegraph: A History of Morse's Invention and Its Predecessors in the United States* (McFarland & Co. 1993); Alvin Harlow, *Old Wires and New Waves: The History of the Telegraph, Telephone and Wireless* (D. Appleton-Century, 1936).

Valuable sources on individuals mentioned in the chapter include: Carlton Mabee, *The American Leonardo: Samuel F. B. Morse* (Knopf, 1943); Paul J. Staiti, *Samuel E. B.*

Morse (Cambridge University Press, 1989); Chester G. Hearn, *Circuits in the Sea: The Men, the Ships, and the Atlantic Cable* (Praeger, 2004); Philip Dorf, *The Builder: A Biography of Ezra Cornell* (Macmillan Co., 1952); Marshall Walter, *Ezra Cornell: 1807–1874: His contributions to Western Union and to Cornell University* (Newcomen Society in North America, 1951); Paul Israel, *Edison: A Life of Invention,* (Wiley, 1998); Ronald William Clark, *Edison: The Man Who Made the Future* (Putnam, 1977); James Crouthamel, *Bennett's New York Herald and the Rise of the Popular Press* (Syracuse University Press, 1989). For the development of the credit-rating industry, see Rowena Olegario, *A Culture of Credit: Embedding Trust and Transparency in American Business* (Harvard University Press, 2006).

CHAPTER THREE

The impact of the railroad on American society and business has been the subject of a vast number of books. Among those I relied upon for this chapter were: *The Railroads: The Nation's First Big Business, Sources and Readings*, compiled and edited by Alfred D. Chandler, Jr., (Harcourt, 1965); Alfred Dupont Chandler, Jr., *Scale and Scope*; George Rogers Taylor and Irene D. Neu, *The American Railroad Network, 1861–1890* (Harvard University Press, 1956); John F. Stover, *The Life and Decline of the American Railroad* (Oxford University Press, 1970); John F. Stover,

American Railroads, (University of Chicago Press, 1997); William Z. Ripley, *Railroads: Finance & Organization* (Longmans Green, 1927); Maury Klein, *Union Pacific* (Doubleday, 1987); Maury Klein, *Unfinished Business: The Railroad in American Life* (University of Rhode Island, 1997); Stephen Ambrose, *Nothing Like It in the World: The Men Who Built the Transcontinental Railroad, 1863–1869* (Simon & Schuster, 2000); Frederick A. Cleveland and Fred Wilbur Powell, *Railroad Finance* (Appleton, 1912); Robert Fogel, *Railroads and American Economic Growth* (Johns Hopkins University Press, 1964); August Veenendaal, *American Railroads in the Nineteenth Century* (Greenwood Press, 2003); Alfred D. Chandler, Jr., and Richard S. Tedlow, *The Coming of Managerial Capitalism: A Casebook on the History of American Economic Institutions* (R.D. Irwin, 1985); and "The Railroad System," *North American Review*, 1867, 476–511.

For the impact of the railroads on the development of Wall Street, I relied on: Robert Sobel, *The Curbstone Brokers: The Origins of the American Stock Exchange* (Macmillan, 1970) and *The Big Board: A History of the New York Stock Exchange* (Free Press, 1965); John Steele Gordon, *The Scarlet Woman of Wall Street* (Weidenfeld & Nicolson, 1988); Edward J. Renehan, Jr., *Dark Genius of Wall Street: The Misunderstood Life of Jay Gould, King of the Robber Barons* (Basic Books, 2005); Ron Chernow, *The House of Morgan* (Touchstone, 1990); and Jean Strouse, *Morgan:*

American Financier (Perennial, 1999); *Capital City: New York City and the Men Behind America's Rise to Economic Dominance, 1860–1900* (Simon & Schuster, 2003); Thomas Kessner and Charles R. Morris, *The Tycoons: How Andrew Carnegie, John D. Rockefeller, Jay Gould and J.P. Morgan Invented the American Supereconomy* (Times Books, 2005).

On the businesses built on the railroads, see: David Nasaw, *Andrew Carnegie* (Penguin, 2006); Cecil C. Hoge, Sr., *Sears and Wards: The First Hundred Years Are the Hardest* (Ten Speed Press, 1988); Gordon Weil, *Sears, Roebuck, USA* (Stein & Day, 1977); John William Ferry, *A History of the Department Store* (MacMillan Co., 1960); *Sears Roebuck Catalogue*, 1897 (Chelsea House Publishers, 1968); Ralph Hower, *History of Macy's in New York, 1858–1919* (Harvard University Press, 1943); *Procter & Gamble: The House that Ivory Built*, by the editors of *Advertising Age* (NTC Business Books, 1988); Davis Dyer, Fred Dalzell, and Rowena Olegario, *Rising Tide: Lessons From 165 Years of Brand Building at Procter & Gamble* (Harvard Business School Press, 2004); and the *International Directory of Company Histories* (St. James Press, 1988).

CHAPTER FOUR

For the financial culture of the 1920s, the crash and the immediate aftermath, valuable resources include: William Leuchtenberg, *Perils of Prosperity, 1914–1932* (University of Chicago Press, 1973); David Greenberg, *Calvin Coolidge* (Henry Holt, 2007); David Cannadine, *Mellon: An American Life* (Knopf, 2006); William K. Klingaman, *1929: The Year of the Great Crash* (Harper & Row, 1989); John Brooks, *Once in Golconda: A True Drama of Wall Street, 1920–1938* (Harper & Row); William Z. Ripley, *Main Street and Wall Street* (Little, Brown, 1929); John Wasik, *The Merchant of Power: Samuel Insull, Thomas Edison, and the Creation of the Modern Metropolis* (Palgrave Macmillan, 2006); John Kenneth Galbraith, *The Great Crash*; and Charles Persons, "Credit Expansions, 1920 to 1929 and its Lessons," *Quarterly Journal of Economics*, November 1930, pp. 94–130. John Raskob's 1929 *Ladies' Home Journal* article appears in Charles Ellis, *The Investor's Anthology: Original Ideas from the Industry's Greatest Minds* (Wiley, 1997).

The best work on the history of the New Deal remains Arthur M. Schlesinger, Jr's three-volume *The Age of Roosevelt* (Houghton-Mifflin, 1957–1960). Domestic anticapitalist sentiment is explored in Alan Brinkley, *Voices of Dissent, Huey Long, Father Coughlins, and the Great Depression* (Vintage Books, 1982). For the financial aftermath and the creation of the New Deal commercial infrastructure, I relied on: Joel Seligman, *The Transformation of Wall Street: A History of the Securities and Exchange Commission and Modern Corporate Finance* (Northeastern University Press, 1995); Ben Bernanke, *Essays on the Great Depression* (Princeton University Press, 2000); C. Lowell

Harriss, *History and Policies of the Home Owners' Loan Corporation* (National Bureau of Economic Research, 1951); James Stuart Olson, *Saving Capitalism: The Reconstruction Finance Corporation and the New Deal, 1933–1940* (Princeton University Press, 1988); Ferdinand Pecora, *Wall Street Under Oath: The Story of Our Modern Money Changers* (Simon & Schuster, 1939); and Robert Sobel, *The Big Board*. The FDIC's website—www.fdic.gov—contains a helpful history of the agency. For anti-FDR revisionism, see Jim Powell, *FDR's Folly: How Roosevelt and His New Deal Prolonged the Great Depression* (Crown Forum, 2003). Charles Kindleberger, *The World in Depression, 1929–1939* (University of California Press, 1973) is a useful comparative study.

For the growth of the lending and investing industries in the 1940s and 1950s, I relied on Lewis Mandell, *The Credit Card Industry: A History* (Twayne Publishers, 1990); Joseph Nocera, *A Piece of the Action: How the Middle Class Joined the Money Class* (Simon & Schuster, 1994); and Edwin Perkins, *Wall Street to Main Street: Charles Merrill and Middle-Class Investors* (Cambridge University Press, 1999).

CHAPTER FIVE

Along with journalistic coverage in business publications, books produced during the 1990s help provide a window into the decade's money culture. They include: George

Gilder, *Telecosm: How Infinite Bandwidth Will Revolutionize Our World Order* (Free Press, 2000); David Elias, *Dow 40,000* (Soaring Eagle Communications, 1998); Charles Kadlec, *Dow 100,000, Fact or Fiction* (New York Institute of Finance, 1999); Bob Woodward, *Maestro: Greenspan's Fed and the American Boom* (Simon & Schuster, 2000); and Justin Martin, *Greenspan: The Man Behind Money* (Perseus, 2000).

The dot-com/fiber-optic bubble inspired a great many books. Among the best are Roger Lowenstein, *Origins of the Crash*, and Om Malik, *Broadbandits: Inside the $750 Billion Telecom Heist* (Wiley, 2003). Other volumes that helped inform this chapter include: Randall Stross, *Eboys: The True Story of the Six Tall Men Who Backed eBay, Webvan, and Other Billion-Dollar Start-Ups* (Ballantine, 2000); Andy Kessler, *Wall Street Meat: My Narrow Escape from the Stock Market Grinder* (Collins, 2004); Charles Gasparino, *Blood on the Street: The Sensational Inside Story of How Wall Street Analysts Duped a Generation of Investors* (Free Press, 2005); John Cassidy, *Dot.Con: The Greatest Story Ever Sold* (HarperCollins, 2002); Nina Munk, *Fools Rush In: Steve Case, Jerry Levin and the Fall of AOL Time Warner* (HarperBusiness, 2004); and Alec Klein, *Stealing Time: Steve Case, Jerry Levin and the Collapse of AOL Time Warner* (Simon & Schuster, 2003).

For the businesses built on the fiber-optic/dot-com infrastructure, I have relied on coverage in *TheStreet.com*,

Business 2.0, *Wired*, *Wall Street Journal*, *Fortune*, *Business-Week*, and *Forbes*. Also: John Battelle, *The Search: How Google and Its Rivals Rewrote the Rules of Business and Transformed Our Culture* (Portfolio, 2005); and David Vise, *The Google Story* (Delacorte Press, 2005).

The consulting firm Telegeography provided data on fiber-optic capacity pricing, and Mary Meeker of Morgan Stanley provided a helpful 2001 presentation on the state of the dot-com market. Web 2.0 executives interviewed for this chapter included Reid Hoffman and Philip Rosedale.

CHAPTER SIX

James Grant's *Grant's Interest Observer* is one of the best sources on the growth and evolution in housing-related credit. Several excellent bloggers cover housing and credit, including Barry Ritholtz (http://thebigpicture.typepad.com), and Jonathan Miller (http://matrix.millersamuel.com). I relied as well on coverage in the *Wall Street Journal*, *New York Times*, and *Barron's*. The Web sites of the National Association of Realtors, the Mortgage Bankers Association, and the Federal Reserve were important sources of data. Mark Zandi of Moody's/Economy.com made available his firm's exhaustive report: *Housing at the Tipping Point: The Outlook for the U.S. Residential Real Estate Market.*

The 2005 paper by Alan Greenspan and James Kennedy, "Estimates of Home Mortgage Originations, Repayments, and Debt on One-to-Four-Family Residences," is on the Fed's Web site. Thomas Philippon and Simi Kedia, "The Economics of Fraudulent Accounting," was published by the National Bureau of Economic Research as a working paper in 2005. Other important articles include Roger Lowenstein, "Who Needs the Mortgage Interest Deduction," *New York Times Magazine*, March 10, 2006, and Jon Gertner, "Chasing Ground," *New York Times Magazine*, October 16, 2005.

Books used include David Lereah, *Are You Missing the Real Estate Boom? The Boom Will Not Bust and Why Property Values Will Continue to Climb Through the End of the Decade—And How to Profit from Them*, and Peter Hartcher, *Bubble Man: Alan Greenspan and the Missing 7 Trillion Dollars* (Norton, 2006).

Interviews conducted for this chapter included: Larry White and Thomas Philippon of New York University, Asha Bangalore of Northern Trust, Mark Zandi of Economy .com, Jan Hatzius of Goldman, Sachs, David Rosenberg of Merrill, Lynch, Robert Shiller of Yale University, and Todd Sinai of the University of Pennsylvania.

CHAPTER SEVEN

I relied on coverage of the alternative energy industry in the *Financial Times*, *Wall Street Journal*, *New York Times*, *Economist*, *Business 2.0*, and *Wired*. Virtually every company

SOURCES

and organization mentioned in the chapter has a Web site
with valuable background and financial data. The writings
of Amory Lovins can be seen on the Web site of the Rocky
Mountain Institute. The Energy Department's Energy Information Agency is an excellent clearinghouse of data on
energy production and supplies and trends in energy use,
and its Alternative Fuels Data Center has information on
state incentives for alternative energy use. The Renewable
Fuels Association provides statistics on the ethanol industry. The Chicago Board of Trade's Web site has data on corn
and ethanol futures. The Pew Center on Global Climate
Change has information on states' renewable energy portfolio standards. And the London-based consulting firm
New Energy Finance provides statistics on global alternative energy investments.

Among the books used for this chapter were Lester
Brown, *Plan B 2.0: Rescuing a Planet Under Stress and a Civ-
ilization in Trouble* (W.W. Norton, 2005); Daniel Esty and
Andrew Winston, *Green to Gold* (Yale University Press,
2006); Travis Bradford, *Solar Revolution: The Economic
Transformation of the Global Energy Industry* (MIT Press,
2006); Al Gore, *An Inconvenient Truth: The Planetary Emer-
gency of Global Warming and What We Can Do About It*
(Rodale, 2006); Matthew Simmons, *Twilight in the Desert:
The Coming Saudi Oil Shock and the World Economy* (Wiley,
2005); and Kenneth Deffeyes, *Beyond Oil: The View from
Hubbert's Peak* (Hill and Wang, 2005).

CHAPTER EIGHT

Books used for this chapter included George Soros, *The Bubble of American Supremacy: Correcting the Misuse of American Power* (PublicAffairs, 2003); Harry S. Dent, *The Next Great Bubble Boom: How to Profit from the Greatest Boom in History, 2005–2009* (Free Press, 2004); David Wiedemer, et. al., *America's Bubble Economy: Profit When It Pops* (Wiley, 2006); Blanch Evans, *Bubbles, Booms and Busts* (McGraw-Hill, 2006); Ron Chernow, *Alexander Hamilton* (Penguin Press, 2004); Benjamin Friedman, *The Moral Consequences of Economic Growth* (Knopf, 2005). Michael Mandel's article appeared in *Business Week* on February 13, 2006. Richardo Haussman and Federico Sturzenegger's paper, "Global Imbalances or Bad Accounting? The Missing Dark Matter in the Wealth of Nations," was published by Harvard University's Center for International Development and John F. Kennedy School of Government Faculty Research Working Paper Series, January 2006.

INDEX